CONTENTS

Barcode: I0151796

THE DISAPPEARING

hope in the
midst of
addiction
and loss

NANCY GRIESHOP, CDP, LPN, LSW

front cover photo: iStock.com/francescoch
back cover photo: iStock.com/holwichaikawee

Printed in the United States of America
Published by Braughler Books LLC., Springboro, Ohio

ISBN: 978-1-970063-79-0

Library of Congress Control Number: 2020918139

Ordering information: Special discounts are available on quantity purchases by bookstores, corporations, associations, and others. For details, contact the publisher at:

sales@braughlerbooks.com
or at 937-58-BOOKS

For questions or comments about this book, please write to:

info@braughlerbooks.com

Braughler™
Books
braughlerbooks.com

ACKNOWLEDGEMENTS

I want to thank my granddaughter, Elizabeth (Riley in the book), for living at my house when she got out of Women's Recovery and helping me understand addiction to the extent that I now do. She trusted me to read her private journal and allow me to put it in print. I have nothing but love, respect, and admiration for her. It was clear to me that she was going through hard times in Florida, but I had no idea of the intensity and violence of her experiences. She will continue to struggle with her issues, but she has an excellent start on her recovery. Great things are coming her way!

I also want to thank my ex-husband, Dale (Joe in this book). He humbly stepped up to the plate and took in three children when he was at the height of his career. Then he retired earlier than he wanted as he came to understand how much more of his time they needed. He is the hero of our family, and will always have a special place in my heart.

Michael Davis is my speech coach. His advice for how to put words and thoughts together for a live presentation, helped me become a better writer. I gained much confidence through knowing him.

Kim White and Nicole Aston, my editors, found typos I missed. They were able to help me soak up thoughts and feelings then wring them out into the words of this book. Their recommendations made this book a better read and helped me find closure in my life. Thanks for taking the time to read the manuscript and advise me.

Sorrow for the loss of my sons lives deep in my soul. I appreciate all my friends and family who continue to reach out to me with their time. When I'm with people and doing things, I feel more alive and happier. I'm sure when we're out and about they think I'm doing well, and that my grief has subsided. I can assure you all that when I'm alone, the slightest memory of my kids can turn my joy of living into deep sadness and dread. Thank you for continuing to take time for me.

I look forward to making new friends along my path going forward. I have a place for you at my supper table.

INTRODUCTION

I'll tell you what.

I never dreamed addiction would infiltrate my family like a big, dirty, rat and wreak havoc in our family like it has. This monster ambles around the world. Looking for its next prey. It studies this person and that one and decides after a moment who it can entrap under its power. Some people don't seem to be quite ready, so it'll come back later and check on them again. It knows that others, after just one sniff, after just one glance they will be ready to take the leap, grab on, and settle into the biggest mistake of their lives. These folks thought that what they saw in this monster was beautiful sights, smells and sounds that they could not have imagined without the drugs. Their emotions soared to the heights of their mind with each new adventure, with each new high. They believed their lives would be so much more than they could experience in their previous tiny, insignificant world.

At first, they thought they had life by the tail and could do extraordinary things forever. Instead they grabbed on to what it really is — the dark, dank underbelly of addiction. And once there, they found it nearly impossible to let go. They had changed. Once engulfed, they didn't know how to get out of the pain and ugliness of this new world they were trapped inside.

This monster has taken the lives of my two sons and has threatened to take my granddaughter's life. It's infuriating. I tried my best to save my sons, yet I was helpless, unable to save them. I have hope for others in my family, who have dabbled in hard drugs and alcohol. I know they have a hard row to hoe.

This book tells stories about my family. About things that happened in my family. About the pain and denial of those who get addicted. And the impatience and fear of loved ones who cannot fix what they witness as their loved one piece by piece, disappears.

QUE SERA SERA

Yesterday I did the eulogy at my son's funeral ceremony. These past three weeks have been unfathomably painful. To add insult to injury, he was my second son to die. My other son died three and a half years ago. Now, two thirds of my kids are dead.

Each of my sons experienced their own addiction hell. Rick, my older son, got coerced into start using drugs when he was eight. Some high school boys befriended him at a park just a couple houses down from where we lived. They gave him a little pocket change as they got him to deliver packets of … something to this house or that one in the neighborhood. They started him off on cigarettes and marijuana. Eventually they got him hooked on heroin when he was a senior in high school.

Things were different with Josh. As far as I know, he never did hard drugs. He just liked his beer, and he had more than his share. He probably started drinking in high school. Like I did. Like nearly everybody I grew up with did. I tried to teach him about alcoholism and the terrible things it does to not only the person addicted, but their entire family.

I'd witnessed the terrible effects of alcoholism firsthand with my brother Alphonse; he was nineteen years older than me and my early memories of him — right through high school — were terrible. When he got home from work, he would sit in the recliner, and sleep (pass out). If I disturbed his sleep in any way that woke him up, I'd get yelled at and he'd whack my hind end. I learned to not disturb him. My brother stopped drinking in his forties and lived a good sober life into his eighties.

The first time I got drunk was when I was four years old. Alphonse got me drunk at our sister's wedding. I had vague memories through my young adulthood that almost seemed more like my imagination. I could see a little girl spinning around in circles. She wore a pretty dress with ruffles and patten leather shoes. As she danced, adults stood around her laughing about how cute she was. I couldn't figure out what this memory was about. I had difficulty with self-confidence and often felt like people were laughing at me when they weren't. Finally, when I was in my forties, Alphonse asked me if I remembered when he got me drunk at our sister's wedding.

I asked, "Did I have a pretty ruffled dress on with patten leather shoes? Was I spinning around in circles? Were people standing around in a circle laughing at me?"

He looked puzzled; I suppose because my memories were so detailed. Then he said, "Yeah, that's what happened."

It felt like a burden was removed from my life. My mind cleared. What a relief to understand what happened! No longer do I feel like people are laughing at me. I now have terrific self-confidence. And I can laugh with people … at me. Very little bothers me anymore.

I told Josh this story, probably more than once. I also told him that there are a lot of alcoholics on my side of the family. Many of them are functional alcoholics. They drink most days and maintain full time jobs. There also are a lot of alcoholics on his dad's side of the family. We had this talk after a family wedding. It was a fairly typical wedding reception. Probably four hundred people invited. Lots of free food and alcohol. Lots of people really drunk. We all got in the car and were ready to go about eleven PM.

Once we were in the van, Joe, my husband, asked, "Why does it smell like a urinal mint in here?"

Josh rather sheepishly started to explain, "Oh, I always try to not have to use the bathroom after eight o'clock when we go to weddings on Mom's side. After eight, the guys in there take a really long time to pee. Well it was after eight and I had to go. A guy in the wedding party waddled in before me. I waited for him to come out. He didn't, so I went in. I really had to go and thought I'd take a chance. The guy was standing there with one hand on the wall above the urinal to steady himself while he was taking a whiz. He fell over backward. When he did, the hand he had on the wall circled down, scooped the urinal mint up in the air, and it landed on the floor beside him."

I asked if the fella stopped peeing.

Josh said, "No. He peed straight up. I jumped over him and slipped in the urinal mint."

We talked a lot about alcoholism on the way home that night. I thought I made an impression on him. I hoped I said enough to keep him from drinking heavy as he got older.

Two years ago, Josh asked me if I remembered the above discussion. I said I remembered it well. He replied, "I should have listened."

By that time, he was hopelessly alcoholic. He had gone through delirium tremors (DTs), had seizures, internal bleeding, and needed to be on a vent twice. All of that within six months. So how did he get there? He was such a loving, fun kid.

Now he's gone and I haven't cried.

WHERE WE BEGAN

Joe, my husband, and I grew up in small town USA. His home town had a population of about 1500. I actually grew up on a farm. Joe had two older sisters and two younger sisters. I had six older brothers and five older sisters. He was the golden boy of his family. I was the baby of the family and was always trying to catch up with eleven older siblings. Trying to make my mark among the gaggle of people I grew up with. We were both raised Catholic. Everybody I knew was pretty much like everybody else I knew. Now that I think about it, I don't remember seeing minorities other than Mexican migrant workers in the fall. They came to pick tomatoes in the many fields in the area. They were doing hard, back breaking work that only some teenagers in the area were able to do. We were not allowed to talk to them, which was a rule I did not question. Some of the boys in my class threw stones at them and laughed as they walked past the school. I didn't understand why they did it. I guess they just felt like they should do it.

There were a lot of similarities between Joe and me, and yet we were different enough to make our relationship interesting. Joe was a free spirit. He has an endearing sense of humor and a quick wit. He also is a great conversationalist so we could talk about a variety of things. I felt good about myself when he was near. His childhood was idyllic from my perspective. There was a community swimming pool a few blocks from his house, and he could go there just about any time he wanted when it was open in the summer. He had a paper route when he was a kid, then when he was old enough, he worked in a factory. He could keep all the money he made.

I worked hard on the farm: hoeing weeds, feeding livestock, milking cows, doing housework. Just things that were perfectly normal for me to do in our family. None of us got paid for our child labor. None of us expected to. But when we went out with friends on the weekend, we were allowed to have a couple bucks from the change cup in the kitchen. The money came from eggs and milk that Mom and Pop sold.

Joe was so different from my brothers — they were all about farming and having fun away from home. Not much fun stuff going on at our house. Nothing was more important than getting the farm work done right and on time. Our farm operated like clockwork. Get up, milk the cows, feed the livestock, take care of planting crops and harvesting, make sure all the equipment worked for the next time it would be needed. Get some sleep. Repeat. Day after day. Month after month. Year after year. I don't know exactly what the boys did when they left the house after their work was done. But I'm pretty sure it involved girls, beer, and driving fast in big cars.

The girls in the family were expected to keep the house running smoothly. That included having meals on the table when the men came in to eat, keeping the house clean, and sewing most of our clothes. Housework was boring to me. I'd rather be outside with the boys and the animals. And if I could drive a tractor, life was sweet.

As I mentioned, we didn't get paid for working. It just was expected we do it. And rare was the time someone got a day off to play or go swimming with friends. None of my brothers were allowed to play in school sports. Too much work to do on the farm. No one went away to college; except my next two older sisters who went to Catholic nursing school. One of my brothers got a scholarship to go to The Ohio State University. He didn't even mention it to Pop. He knew he wouldn't be allowed to go.

I wanted to be a teacher, but Pop told me I would not be going to go to college, because, "You might learn stuff that you shouldn't know."

He said it in German, so I knew he meant it. Instead, I went to a technical school and majored in nursing. My plan was to get a job as an LPN and go back to college. I didn't end up as a teacher. Instead I went into social work, which seemed more like a vocation than a profession. I was living and working in a profession that defined my values.

A while back I told my sisters and sisters-in-law that when I was a kid and realized I couldn't become a priest; I became a social worker. There was at least one pffit and probably some eye rolling coming from those who heard me.

I explained, "No really. I used to practice saying Mass upstairs. I had cardboard (probably from silk-stocking packages) that I made some prayer cards out of, and scribbled on them to make them look like the prayer cards the priest read from at Mass. I knew all the Latin prayers by heart. I used a little votive candle for my chalice. I wanted to keep this sacred piece that in my mind held the body of Christ, in a special place while I wasn't using it for Mass. I found just the place for it. A blue box in my sister's closet that had some soft, cotton like something in the bottom."

By this time everyone in the room had a bit of a questioning, what-is-she-talking-about expression on their faces. So, I wrapped up my story by saying, "I finally quit this very solemn ceremony after my sister Miriam cornered me, seeming upset for some reason."

She looked at me and said, "Nancy, I wished you'd stop putting your candle in my Kotex box."

I didn't even know what a Kotex was. I stopped putting my chalice in that box. I still have it on my roll top desk.

• • •

It was kind of weird to be the youngest in the family. My earliest memory of the supper table included eleven people sitting there. My three oldest siblings were married and gone before I have any memory of them being home. The supper table was organized by chaos. Five boys. Four girls. Mom and Pop. It was crowded. We all got enough food. Nobody got more than their share. Meals always included meat, potatoes, vegetable, bread, fresh milk, and dessert. The thing that was weird to me about being the youngest, was that the number of people at the table decreased as my siblings got married and moved out on their own. I missed them. They didn't come back to eat with me or give me a hard time except when they came to visit as "company." They usually came with their kids, and I would have someone to play with and boss around. It kind of sucked when me, Mom, Pop and occasionally Alphonse were the only ones left at the table. I felt a bit uncomfortable with it being so few of us there. I still want more people in my life these days. I don't seem to be able to fill up my supper table. No matter how many friends l have or people I know.

Joe and I got acquainted when I was a junior in high school, and he was going to college. We generally met at a dance on Sunday at the Carousel Ballroom near Celina, Ohio. Beer was easy to get even for those of us underage. It's what we did. There was always a live band and the cover charge was $1. Beer was a quarter a cup. We all had plenty of that — even if we were only sixteen. Two dollars provided everything we needed for four or five hours of entertainment. It was so fun. We danced the night away. My girlfriends and I went out on Wednesdays, Fridays, and Sundays. Saturdays were date nights. It's kind of amazing that we all got good grades and were active in church groups. We didn't get in any trouble, for the most part.

The economy was bad in the early to mid-1970s. There were no good jobs in the area unless you lived on a farm. Well, I could always get a job as a nurse. But Joe had a degree in psychology, with no prospects of working in that arena back home. We both were envious of my sister Ginger who married an Air Force officer. They were traveling all over the country. It just seemed like Ginger and Jim had such an idyllic life. Joe joined the Air Force as the Vietnam conflict was coming to an end. The whole world seemed messed up and here we go, getting married and leaving home in search of adventures. I was twenty. Joe was twenty-two. What were we thinking?

Joe was stationed at Lackland Air Force Base in San Antonio, Texas. Wow that was a change of pace! I grew up in a very soup bowl kind of lifestyle. Everybody pretty much looked and prayed like me. San Antonio was mostly minority — Mexican and African American. I figured out they were good people for the most part and I made friends with a lot of them. There were a lot of Catholics there, but I got a glimpse of Southern Baptists and their belief systems. Quite an eye-opener. I don't think I ever convinced one of the Baptists I worked with that Catholics really don't have tails, like her momma said.

I loved so many things about the culture there: festivals, cowboys and southern charm. I was in heaven by many aspects of this new adventure. Yet I had a difficult time adjusting to being gone from home for long periods of time. When we were in Ohio, I could always run home to be around family and farm life. In Texas we couldn't even afford for me to call and talk to my mom now and then. Joe made $250 semi-monthly as an Airman. Our rent was $100 a month. Our utilities, food, car payment, and insurance had to come out of what was left. For months we didn't have furniture because we couldn't afford it. We sat home and played cards or played tennis. Stuff that was free. Eventually we started making friends and had things to do socially. Life was so simple then. Drugs and hard liquor did not enter the picture. For one thing we had no money for that stuff, even if we would have been interested. I started to believe that I could do anything I wanted to do. As long as I didn't want to do something I couldn't afford.

After three years of living in San Antonio, we felt ready to start a family. We were able to buy a three-bedroom house and move into it with our baby, Rick. Things had really changed for us to be able to afford all this. But I ended up being a stay at home mom because we had but one car and I couldn't wrap my head around putting my baby in day care. That just wasn't something we did where I'm from. Moms stayed home with their babies. So we were down my income, and I was going nuts staying home. I needed a little more action than feeding a baby and changing diapers. I started working at a hospital about one mile from where we lived. And Joe worked about three miles from home. It was awesome as things worked out.

I got pregnant again.

Josh was born twenty-three months after Rick. It was easier for me to get used to having a second son than getting used to the first one. Josh was such a cute chubby baby. Plus, I was in labor less than three hours with him. Labor with Rick was agonizing for twelve hours. Of course, Josh made up for it by being allergic to milk and had colic nearly every night for three hours — times three months. It was exhausting.

I was so ready to get back to Ohio by this time. I wanted to be close to our families. And I wanted our kids to know their cousins and my parents who were in their seventies already. I wanted to raise them with the same values I was raised with, and to me, that meant getting back to where I was raised. It made sense emotionally. Financially, nope. We were doing fine in Texas, but to move to Ohio. Hmm. Maybe we should have thought about it a minute longer. Interest rates were thirteen to seventeen percent. Inflation five to nine percent. Eww! The house we bought was $37,000.00. Nothing fancy. House payment $600.00. Joe made $606.00 biweekly. Things were tight.

So, of course, we had another baby when Josh was nearly two years old. Sophie has always been the joy of my life. And from the time she was born, she was a game changer for her brothers. They were gentle with her at first, but once she was able to walk, bam! She became a target for their affection. Well they weren't exactly affectionate with her, but she certainly got a lot of attention from them. Unwanted attention, to be more clear. She'd often hide very quietly behind the couch, to avoid said "attention."

Sophie complained about the treatment she got from her brothers sometimes. I figured; how bad can it be? She only had but two brothers; I had six. And some of them were rough on me. I generally shrugged off her complaints and told her they'd make her tough. Then when I had each of the boys alone, I'd try to convince them to take it easy on their baby sister. She was a light weight and couldn't stand up for herself. Nothing changed. They still gave her a hard time. Sophie grew up to be the toughest chick I ever knew. She's strong willed, has a stronger character, and is unwavering in her desire to move ahead. The weird part is that in her toughness, she remains elegant and sophisticated. At least from a distance!

Rick

Rick loved his little brother from the first second they met. He protected Josh and taught him so many things when they were little. Things were a lot different by the time they were in high school. The first car they got was an old deserted Dodge Aries. They dug it out of the snow in Joe's parents back yard and took it home. It needed a little work. They were creative with their repairs. The gear shifter thing was held together with popsicle sticks, a vice grip, and duct tape. The first date Josh had with Audrey, she had to get up under the hood to get the car from reverse to drive. And she still married him!

The rift between the brothers apparently started because of a car. Josh found a canary yellow 1969 Dodge Firebird and was trying to get up the nerve to ask me for help getting it. Rick had the nerve, and I helped him get the loan not knowing Josh saw it first. It seems Josh never forgave him for that. How silly! I just heard this part of the story a few years ago. It still seems dumb to me to hold a grudge like that. A grudge between two brothers that lasted a lifetime.

Rick married a different kind of girl. Ashley had a troubled youth. I heard she was molested by an uncle when she was but a child, dropped out of school by the time she was fifteen. She was using opiates — she liked her Vicodin — and weed when she and Rick met. They married young; Rick was twenty and Ashley was eighteen. They had twins, Gunner and Riley, nine months after they married.

They had no money and having kids so soon didn't help a bit financially. They moved around a lot. Rick had a hard time getting to work because Ashley had a hard time taking care of the kids. The abuse she experienced when she was a child, resulted in some mental and emotional challenges which made taking care of kids difficult. They were good at making babies. Hunter was born five years after the twins, and Katie came two years after that. It seems like Rick and Ashley had enough money for drugs, as they continued to use them through all this. Of course, there may have been some other ill-advised activities going on all the while.

Children's services were involved from the time the twins were two. They were homeless several times and in foster homes several more times. When the twins were ten all the kids had been placed permanently in other homes — Gunner, Riley, and Hunter went to live with Joe, and it continues to break my heart, that Katie was adopted out. It was more than we could do to try to raise Katie. She continues to do well in her adoptive family. I haven't seen her for eleven years. I sure hope we'll find each other at some point. I want her to know that I love her, miss her and think about her every day.

Ashley dealt with losing custody of all her kids by numbing herself against the pain. She mixed up some drugs and accidently overdosed under a tree in her dad's front yard. What an emptiness that left in her kids — especially Riley. The pain of losing her mom when she was ten years old continues to wreak havoc in her life. I'm not sure how it impacted the boys. Hunter doesn't talk about her. Gunner doesn't even remember her.

We didn't know where Rick was for six years after Ashley died. We didn't know if he was dead or alive. Then he contacted Joe.

He was clean of cocaine, heroin, and all the other hard drugs he'd been using. But he still used beer and weed. He wanted to get back with his kids. That happened and we had three years of getting to know each other again. By that time, Rick really seemed to have gotten his stuff together. Hunter was living with him, and he was engaged to be married. So, one day in May 2016, he dived into the swimming pool in his back yard, and hit his forehead on the bottom, which resulted in him breaking his neck. He drowned as his fiancé futilely, and there alone, was helpless to save him.

A new overwhelming sense of abandonment for his kids. It could scar them forever.

Josh's Youth

Josh was such a cute little kid in grade school. So lovable, huggable, sweet. And yet he could tease the crap out of his little sister, Sophie, who just wanted to be left alone.

He loved to be active. I was forever playing catch with him in our back yard. Softball, baseball, football. Joe took care of the game of basketball. He presided over that. I would generally get a bit frustrated playing roundball with Joe; he tended to come up with new rules as we played which seemed to always help his score. When we played football, I got to be a pretty good quarterback, at least by my standards. Josh's secret play as a running back with the pee wee team he was on, was the button hook to get the extra two points following a touchdown. He would run straight out five or ten yards, cut outside and I would have the ball exactly over his shoulder when he turned his head to look for it, just as planned. He was so mad after the final tournament in sixth grade. He kicked the tires before he got in the car. I asked what was wrong.

He said, "You should have let me play in fourth grade." Well too late.

Josh loved to eat fresh vegetables one of his favorite snacks was carrots dipped in French dressing. He would eat carrots every day after school. Eating hard vegetables should have stopped when he got braces on his teeth. He ate them anyway and had to get the bands replaced frequently. By the time he'd had them on longer than anyone else in the orthodontist's practice, the whole braces thing was getting old. He had a quizzical expression on his face after one of his many appointments. He got in the car and asked what it meant when the hygienist told him he was "spinning his wheels." I laughed and explained it's like the wheels were going around fast but the car's not moving anywhere. He must have gotten the hint because he stopped eating fresh carrots, and soon thereafter had the braces removed. That's probably about the time he started smoking.

The smoking thing I never understood. All my brothers smoked. It was what they did. It was totally acceptable, even around the supper table. They would light up with a silver flip top, flint lighter. I never saw a cigarette ash or butt anywhere in the kitchen. Nope. They all rolled up the bottom of their jeans pants and flipped their ashes in those cuffs. It was such a 60's West Side Story thing to do.

I heard about smoking corn silk when I was a kid, and I had to try it. I wrapped some of it inside of a bit of newspaper and lit it up. Yuck! I'm pretty sure I turned several shades of green. It didn't appeal to me at all. I did enjoy watching it burn holes in the hem of my dress. I didn't have the courage to explain that to Mom. Another time I tried to smoke a real cigarette when I was a senior in high school. I was at a dance and one of my classmates gave me one. I lit it up and heard one of my friends laugh at me. Well, I didn't like for people to laugh at me (recall — little girl in a pretty dress, spinning in circles). I never lit up another one.

But with Josh, it was quite another thing. He apparently liked to smoke. As a general rule I stayed out of his bedroom because I didn't like to get grossed out. (Once Rick had taken a rat home from school. A big rat. At least ten inches long, with a tail at least that long at the back end of it. He got it home by slipping it down his jacket sleeve. It was brown and white, and his name was Grover. I found Grover in the aquarium that used to house fish. I about wet myself when I first came upon it. It took a while, but Rick finally got rid of it. I think he decided to do something else with Grover as his lower canine teeth were growing up and around in a circle — past his nose, around by his eyes, and beginning to reach the ridge of his nose. Not too much longer and poor Grover would be breathing with his teeth stuck in his nostrils. Another time I found the aquarium filled with mice. Little gray and white mice of different generations. Funny thing how mice reproduce at an astronomical rate. And like cats, the male will eat their young so he can mate again. I found many tails and feet that were not connected to any other body parts. Just plain gross. Rick got rid of the mice after I told him we would not get a dog as long as there were mice in the house. The mice disappeared the next day. I wasn't sure what he did with them, until my neighbor asked me if I had mice in my back yard, too.)

Anyway, one day I decided to go up to Josh's bedroom, just because. OMG what a mess. I picked up an empty popcorn bag that had dozens of cigarette butts in it. Plus, there were butts all over the floor. I told him that if he decided to spend his money on cigarettes, he certainly had enough money to buy his own clothes. So, I didn't buy him new school clothes that fall. By November it was getting a little cold and the only clothes that fit him were summer clothes. I think he wanted long pants to wear as he never liked to be cold. He said he already quit smoking, so could I take him shopping, please. I did. And I'm pretty sure he continued to smoke anyway.

• • •

One of the very best things I ever did with Josh was to take him to a dude ranch in Montana. I had gone to the same place with a friend two years earlier. So, the summer he was sixteen, I arranged for Josh, Rick, and my friend Esther to go to Shivley ranch about fifty miles from Billings as the crow flies. But by following the dirt roads it took about three hours to drive around the Indian reservation. Rick was gone when it was time for us to leave. I was on a deadline. We had to get going as I was going to drop Sophie off at Joe's sister's house in Iowa, then I'd go the rest of the way with Josh. I called all of Rick's friends. I drove around to many of their houses. No one knew a thing about him or what he was doing that morning. (Right.)

On the way out, Josh and I stopped at the Badlands, the Wall, and Mount Rushmore. The Badlands were awesome. I thought Josh fell in a crater or something at one point. I just couldn't find him. Yet around the corner there he was, grinning from ear to ear. He loved that place. The Harleys were things of beauty at the Wall. Mount Rushmore was very impressive.

That night we stayed in a hotel. I went out and got a six pack of beer. When I got back in our room, Josh said, "Can't you go one day without that stuff?"

"I'm on vacation and I want a beer and relax a bit after all that driving. You want one?"

He took one and poured it down his throat before I had half mine gone. I was a little surprised. Actually, my eyebrows were up around my hairline. I looked over at him, and said, "Well that's not the first beer you've had!"

He took another one. Down the hatch it went. We stopped at two each. I didn't think too much of the incident. Afterall, I'd had some beers by the time I was his age.

* * *

Josh always was a loyal friend. He had this one friend in grade school, Jeremy. They played on weekends. Josh never asked to go to any other friends, and Jeremy was the only friend he had over at our house. Unpredictably, the friendship was suddenly over. Josh didn't want to talk about it. He sulked over it for weeks. We tossed a lot of balls to each other in the back yard during that time.

His next friends were of a different nature. Mark was born into a very rich family. He had his own credit card when he was a sophomore in high school, and really ticked off some guys when he would buy their girlfriends expensive jewelry. That broke up several perfectly good relationships. My gosh the cars he had. A Cadillac with hydraulics on every wheel — he'd make them all go up and down in different patterns. It was very creative, and funny when he came to pick Josh up for school. The neighbors complained about it, so I had to put a stop to it. Their complaints had more to do with the speaker system than the hydraulics. Mark turned up the speakers so loud the neighbors' windows rattled as he approached and drove by. It was kind of funny, but we had quiet neighbors. They didn't seem to think it was funny.

Josh's other new BFF was Finley. Finley's parents took the two boys to their first concert — the Rolling Stones. Now how can anything compare to that? Finley was a bit of an odd sort, too. Quiet, unassuming. And one of the funniest people I ever knew. Such a dry sense of humor. And kind of dumb. The two of them came upon a Bosnian security group when the peace talks were in town. They tried to interact with the foreigners, you know, make friends. Instead they nearly got arrested or shot.

Another time they went shopping at Wal Mart, and basically just walked around, killing time. They didn't buy a thing. And when they were leaving, the alarms came on. They just knew the alarms did not pertain to them. They didn't even buy anything. Seconds later, the two boys were escorted into a security area in the back of the building. They were ordered to empty their pockets. Finley had CDs, tools for fixing cars, silverware, jewelry, toys, and … a car battery. Josh said he watched in disbelief as Finley filled up an eight-foot-long table with things he had packed into his coat pockets. Josh had pocket lint to add to the treasure. Finley died of an overdose a few years back.

Josh and Audrey started grade school together. A few years ago, I found a picture of their second-grade class. Josh was standing behind Audrey with his hand on the back of her chair. They were so cute. They started dating in high school. They moved in together the fall after they graduated from high school. And married in the Bahamas a year later. They were each twenty years old. They were so in love. What a fun, happy couple they were.

Sophie

Ahhh, Sophie. So filled with gentle strength. So wise. Before she was born, I thought I knew the love of a child. Once she was born, I knew that a baby girl adds to the depth of bonding of mother to a child that a baby boy generally does not provide. The strand that binds baby to mother to grandmother to great-grandmother — and on and to the first mother to give birth to a girl — is so special. Males seem to attempt to complete their lives when they fall in love with someone and move on from their mom. Females seem to get closer to their mothers as they move on with their lives into adulthood. Then the strand of life and love continues as they have children of their own.

When Sophie was born, I fell in love all over again. It was a deeper love than I could experience with the boys. She was such a delicate baby, compared to her brothers who popped out ready to take on the world. She took her time. She would sit back and watch before making her move, which was often to turn tail and hurry away. She took on her world at her pace. When she was done using the bottle, she just wouldn't take it. She practiced standing up for weeks before she tried to walk; crouch down, stand up, repeat. And potty training? One day she used the toilet and didn't want a diaper on ever again. She found a way to capture her solitude when her brothers became too rambunctious — she'd take paper and crayons behind the couch and draw all the while humming possibly to drown out the sounds of her brothers.

Every time I see the first star of the evening, I have warm memories of Sophie from when she was a toddler. I can't help but smile even today when I see that first star in the twilight of the evening. I wanted to help Sophie feel like the princess she was to me. The powerful princess who had the stars in the sky at her beck and call. So I'd carry her on my hip and walk around in our back yard after the sun went down.

I would point to a star I saw and say to her, "Oh there's the first star of the night. Let's see if we can sing out some more stars."

She would hone in on where I was pointing, and smile.

We would sing a silly little ditty, "Singa, singa, singa," over and over. It worked! Every single time we sang it, more and more stars came out in the evening sky. As they came out, she would giggle with her delicate finger pointing at each new star that suddenly appeared. She looked in my eyes with so much wonderment in hers. I hoped she would grow up to feel superhuman, knowing she could sing out the stars.

When she was four, Sophie started calling me by my first name. I remember the day well. We were at a church picnic up where I grew up. I had adults to talk to for a change and enjoyed taking advantage of the opportunity. Sophie repeatedly tried to get my attention as I ignored her.

"Mom." No response.

"Mommy." I might have taken a sip of my drink.

"Mother." That was different.

"Mrs. Welkamp." She's getting serious.

"Nancy!"

That got it. As it turns out she had to go potty. Like, now. She called me Nancy from then till after she became the mother of a little girl. Now we're back to "Mom" most of the time. Generally, it's Nanc only when I've done something really dumb and she's about to let me know how she feels about it.

Sophie was able to figure some things out much quicker than the boys. One evening everybody was in bed but me. I was enjoying the TV show I wanted to watch, without interruption. That didn't last long. First Josh came downstairs to go potty. Then he crawled up on my lap and snuggled in.

I looked at him and hugged him, and said, "You're my favorite six-year-old in the whole world."

He grinned from ear to ear with so much love in his eyes and said, "I know, Mommy." And he ran upstairs.

In no time at all Rick came running down and used the toilet. Then he crawled up on my lap snuggled in. I looked at him and hugged him and said, "You're my favorite eight-year-old in the whole world."

He grinned and looked at me and said, "I know, Mommy." Then off to bed he trotted.

Eventually, Sophie came out of her room to go potty. Then she crawled up on my lap. She never did really snuggle as much as Josh did at that time.

I looked at her and said, "You're my favorite four-year-old in the whole world."

She looked at me with not so much of a loving look in her eyes, more of a "yeah right" look. I tried to stifle a guffaw, as I heard these words come out of her face, "Oh, you say that to all of us."

She got down off my lap and marched straight to bed, making her point more unmistakable with each stomp of her dainty little feet.

. . .

Sophie spent most of her time with Josh during her early years. They interacted on equal footing. At least that's what I thought. Josh loved to tease her, to the point she would call out for help. I probably took her side more often than she deserved. She would complain about something that she said he was doing, and I would yell at Josh. When I told him to stop teasing her so much, he explained he had to do it because, "I'm good at it."

I'm pretty sure she took advantage of my standing up for her and not him because a couple times she'd start yelling at Josh when he wasn't even in the same room. After that happened a couple times, I finally said, "Girl, you're on your own. You go figure it out."

You can bet Josh toughened her up. He taught her sports by watching baseball and football games with her. She probably knew more about the rules and strategies by the time she was in junior high than I ever will. She learned how to stand up for herself through all the times he picked on her. She still stands up for the underdog and doesn't let anybody push her around. I wonder how many raises she got in the past several years by threatening to quit her job when she felt taken advantage of by management. I love seeing what a strong woman she has become.

Sophie took a while to warm up to Rick. There were times she wanted to hang with him. So one day Rick played barber with Sophie when she was four. Of course, he was the barber, she was the customer. He must have gone on strike halfway through creating her new doo. She had no bangs, shoulder length hair in the back and on the right side of her head. I felt my face get red when I saw the left side. It was cut, straight across, above her ear. Ugh!

As the years went by, Rick had an influence on Sophie. In a more of a detrimental way. They got really close during the time drugs started to have a strangle hold on Rick. Rick coaxed her into withdrawing hundreds of dollars from her savings account when she was maybe twelve or thirteen. I didn't hear about it till years after he moved out of the house.

By the time she was in junior high, Rick was a super cool mystery to her. He used her to do his bidding, but she didn't care. She finally liked the attention she got from him. Apparently, he once had her drive his car before she had her license because he was afraid he'd lose his. He also got Sophie to tow his Firebird down SR 35 with her little Grand Am. And of course, the boys had parties when Joe and I had a night out on the town. They were all teenagers, and were old enough to know better, young enough to not care. It was scary for her because "those guys were old and drunk."

⋅ ⋅ ⋅

Through all the stupid stuff Rick did, all the ways he hurt all of us, Sophie was so supportive of me. She would ask me how I was doing. And try to get me to talk about some of the stuff she knew was bothering me, and I just couldn't put it to words. It was like

I was living with a dome of static, surrounding me everywhere I went. I couldn't talk to anyone, family, or friends, about how I was doing because I didn't know. I went to counseling, sometimes alone, sometimes with Rick, sometimes with Joe. I went to Al-anon meetings thinking maybe Rick was drinking. I tried to understand what was going on with him. Nothing made sense. Why was he getting into so much into trouble?

One day Sophie was trying to comfort me when she was in maybe eighth grade. I was so distraught about things Rick was doing. She got my attention when she said, "You can no more change him into being more like me than you can change me into being more like him."

Like I said, she's one of the wisest people I've ever known.

The competition among my kids was ... weird. They competed at being the first in the car when we went somewhere, the first to finish dinner, the first to take a bath. The boys were good at softball. And so was Sophie. She and I practiced in the back yard a lot, but not nearly as much as Josh and I did. It was fun. By the time she was in third grade, I was throwing the softball to her as hard as I threw it to Josh. Joe poked his head out the patio door one day and told me to not throw it so hard to her. She is a girl after all. Well that ticked me off. I kept throwing the ball hard. She never missed. She's still good at softball. And no balls get past her when she's on the field.

All the kids went to public school. When Sophie finished her eighth grade, she insisted on going to the local Catholic school. She saw this as a way to avoid the status of "Little Welkamp" she had in the public school. She didn't want the burden of being their sister, living with their reputation hovering all about her. Going to a different school was a change of pace. She learned that while public school kids preferred beer and stronger alcohol as their drug of choice, these Catholic school kids preferred pot and other street drugs. The parking lot by the football field was known as "the back forty" and that's where drugs were exchanged for money and other favors. Somehow, she didn't join in with that activity. Thank goodness.

Sophie completed freshman and sophomore years at the Catholic school. She knew several kids who died during this time, in fact I think she was a pall bearer for five of them. She took the city bus to some of the funerals. It was a different kind of life. She went to places near the high school, that would not have been available to her had she continued in the public school. One of those places was a pool hall. It was across the street from the high school. Apparently, she was getting good at shooting some stick. One day she came home and explained that some older fellas (probably eighteen or nineteen!) challenged her to a game.

She looked them straight in the eye and said, "Sure. But you better first put a book in your pants."

They had puzzled looks on their faces and asked why.

"So it doesn't hurt so bad when I kick your ass" was her straight up, serious response.

They tucked tail and left. I could not laugh hard enough when she told me about it.

* * *

The boys grew up and left home. Rick was married. Josh moved in with Audrey. Sophie continued to be able to figure me out more and more. For about a year, she would ask me practically every week if Joe and I were getting a divorce. At first, I wasn't even considering that. But Joe and I were drifting apart. It was like we were living in alternate universes. Sometimes I didn't recognize him when he was standing right in front of me. She picked up on that way before getting a divorce was part of my thinking.

When I finally told her a divorce was probably going to happen, Sophie immediately said, "I'm staying with you. I don't care if you live in Fort Loramie or in Grandpa's old house, I want to stay with you." That was surprising and comforting. I really couldn't imagine either scenario playing out. I didn't want to live in either place by that time.

. . .

Once Joe and I were separated, Sophie and I had some great times together. I got her and her friends to play darts. I even subbed on her team, Random Play. I'm grinning ear to ear just thinking about it now. She and her best friend, Ella, went to some of my dart tournaments. One of them, in Chicago, is quite memorable. Ella and Sophie got there late on Friday. They were a big hit on the dance floor but didn't partake in the clothes optional party that continued all night long.

Her friends came over quite a bit to party in our basement where they played mostly foosball and flip cup. She wouldn't let any of them smoke in the house. I admired her for that, because at the time, smoking in restaurants and other public places was still legal, acceptable, and happened regularly.

One day we had a serious discussion about her friends. She was a bit distraught as she explained that I was her friends' (the boys) MILF.

I was puzzled and asked, "What's a MILF?"

Response: "Mom I'd like to f--k."

She looked totally disgusted with her friends as she explained. "Really?"

"Yeah. Isn't that terrible?"

I paused a little longer. Then I smiled real big and said, "Cool!"

She was embarrassed and so mad because I kind of liked the designation. They thought I was hot. She left the room. Seems like I was never included when she went out with her friends after that, nor did she have parties at our house. Hmmm? Wonder why.

. . .

Sophie spent her last two years of high school at the county career center, majoring in auto mechanics. She didn't want to go into anything having to do with working in an office because she, "wasn't going to photocopy anything for any man."

In the early weeks of school that fall, she illustrated to me what the boys were like in her class. They were not respectful of her.

One of the boys demonstrated to her how she would look better on top of the hood rather than working under it. That ticked me off, and I told her that was sexual harassment and if she didn't feel like reporting it, I would. She begged me to not get involved with this, as she took care of it. She never told me exactly what happened, other than what she said to him was a lot worse than what he said to her. That's my girl. Thanks to Josh for teaching her how to cuss! And take a punch. And give a punch.

She ended up becoming a master mechanic. Hard to imagine, I know. That beautiful, young woman was a grease monkey. She worked at a local car dealership. The guys gave her a hard time, of course. She was determined to move up the ladder and get out from under the hood. So finally, one day she talked her boss into letting her be a service writer. Score! Things were going good. She didn't have to do any dirty work. All she had to do was sign people up for repairs to their cars. Then when the repairs were complete, she would call them up to the desk and take their payment.

In the afternoon she got to a ticket she hadn't written. She got on the PA system that announced to the entire business complex, "Dick Wacker your car is ready. Please come to the service desk."

She went about her business. Nobody came up to claim the car. She announced again a few minutes later. Louder and more clearly, "Mr. Dick Wacker your car is ready. Please come to the service desk."

She again went about her work. No one showed up at her desk. She was about to announce his name a third time, when a skinny little fella came up to her desk and said, "The name is Richard Wratcher."

The mechanics working in the bays were falling down laughing. That might have been the impetus she needed to keep working toward getting double majors in communication and strategic leadership. And getting out of the grease monkey business.

• • •

Sophie had her first grand mal seizure at this job. She was at her lunch break and walking back to the shop when she fell over backwards, seizing for several minutes. I caught up with her in the emergency room. She was scared. I felt deflated, as I thought back across the many, many seizures Joe had. I witnessed a lot of them. They scared me. The cause of them was low blood sugar. Whenever he had them, his blood sugar was less than thirty. Since Joe didn't remember what it was like when he had them, he denied that they even happened. It was infuriating. He didn't eat the way he should. He didn't take his meds the way he should. This went on for thirty years till he finally admitted he had "epileptic-like seizures."

I braced myself as Sophie went through the testing that determined that her seizures were caused by low blood sugar as well. There were now four generations of Welkamps with low blood sugar and seizures. I didn't know if I'd be able to deal with what I anticipated would be my life — waiting anxiously for the next seizure. She felt my distancing and finally after weeks of this, she said, "Nanc, I need your help with this. I'm not Dad. I want to get these seizures under control."

Finally, I realized that distancing was exactly what I was doing. I was fighting the last war, so to speak. I was remembering my struggles dealing with Joe's denial of his problems, and I didn't want to get the push back from Sophie like I did from Joe. Clearly Sophie was not Joe. She wanted to address her seizure problem head on, and make sure she never had another one. So different from Joe.

. . .

I loved her next job. She had to travel to the west coast and to different spots nearer home. What I liked about it was I got to travel with her to West Virginia, Oregon, California, Las Vegas, and Anchorage. She didn't like it because the job was doing inspections at public transportation places. The thing she inspected was the way urine specimens to check for drugs were collected and processed. Imagine doing that in places as varied as

San Francisco, Anchorage, and remote Indian reservations in the Rocky Mountains. What an oxymoron. My little girl was standing up to big burly men and calling them out on the inconsistencies in their paperwork. She is the same person who couldn't say the word "bra" till she was out of high school.

This job was definitely anxiety producing for her. And she's been familiar with anxiety for her whole life. Two older brothers and the crap they put her through. The seizures. So many challenging things totally out of her control. In this job she travelled alone nearly all the time. The anxiety hit her often when she drove to her next job site.

One day it hit hard as she was heading to Athens, Ohio to do an inspection. Anxiety was high when she was between Springfield and Columbus, Ohio. She called me and said she felt like she was going to crash because she couldn't focus on driving. I tried to get her to pull over, and I'd go get her. She said she'd drive home instead of continuing on her way. Then she called and said once she turned around and drove a while, she felt better so headed toward Columbus again. A little while and she called and said she couldn't focus well enough to drive. Back and forth she went. Then I didn't hear from her, and she didn't answer the phone for a couple hours. Now *my* anxiety was going up. Finally she called. She decided to just drive to where she needed to be. She made it. Dang it, girl.

Her next job, which is the job she has now is with a government contractor. Her orientation to this giant corporation was in Washington, DC. If you do a lot of travelling, you know that many flights going to DC have a layover in Atlanta. And there's often stormy weather over Atlanta. This flight was no exception. Sophie's plane flew for hours over Atlanta, till the storm abated, and could finally land. She had to transfer to another plane, then fly to D.C. She got to her hotel in the middle of the night, lay down without being able to relax, and then took off just a few hours later for her orientation program, in another hotel.

About 10:30 in the morning I got a voice mail from her. "Nanc, I'm in the ER at George Washington hospital. I had a seizure."

What??? ! ! ! No phone number to call. No "I'm fine." And now her phone was dead. Crap.

I called many numbers till I finally got through to the correct desk and Sophie got on the phone. She answered and told just a little more about the seizure. First the crazy flight. No sleep. Nothing to eat since the day before. What happened was she was in the orientation class and stood up to answer a question. After a few seconds of talking, she fell over backward.

Then woke up in an ambulance with paramedics asking stupid questions, like, "What day is it?" and "Where are you?" and "Where do you live?" You know, questions she had no idea how to answer.

I said I'd be right there before it occurred to me that I probably wouldn't get there for ten hours. Then she said the doctor was in, and she'd call me right back. We hung up.

I waited and waited. And worried and worried. "Right back" happened on her lunch break the next day. She had been released from ER shortly after we talked. She didn't know about any tests that might have been done. She was put in a cab and left the hospital. She couldn't remember her hotel and didn't have her papers with her. They drove around till they came to a hotel that looked familiar. It was the right one! She went to bed and slept till the next morning when she got up and returned to the orientation program. I can't imagine how embarrassed she was. She knew she had to take control of the situation, as she didn't like the attention and questions people were asking.

So she said, "I'm fine. I'll get through this. I just don't know how I'm going to explain the rug burns on my back to my husband."

That got some laughs and she survived the day.

Just to give an idea of how little attention Sophie wants, she got her graduate degree from Cornell University last summer and didn't even tell anybody. But that was last summer. And last summer was very distracting, as you'll see.

. . .

So many things Sophie did were so different from the way the boys did them. They didn't date many girls and got married before they turned twenty-one. Sophie had a generous helping of boyfriends and waited to get married till she was twenty-six. The boys had some interesting jobs as they tried to figure out who they were. Sophie spotted good jobs and went for them. Now she's making her mark. The boys started using drugs and / or alcohol by the time they graduated from high school and kept using lots as time went on. Sophie never overdid it, as far as I know. She was often the designated driver. Even on long vacations with her friends, she drove the whole time so her friends could party on.

. . .

The man she married, is perfect for her. Jimmy is a hard worker, mild mannered, devoted to Sophie and their kids, crazy in love with his wife, and respectful of me. Sophie called me the evening she got engaged to him. Jimmy had prepared an exquisite candle-light dinner for her. After desert, he got down on his knee and popped the question. She happily said, "Yes!"

I was ecstatic when she called to tell me. After I shared her glee, I asked her to put Jimmy on the phone. I congratulated him and said I could not imagine anyone better suited to be Sophie's husband.

Then I added, "If you ever do anything to hurt her, I will kick your ass."

Very solemnly he responded, "I know that's what took me so long to ask her."

We never talked about our conversation till about five years later, when he asked if I remembered it.

I said, "Yes I do. And I haven't had a single reason or urge to kick your ass. Yet."

. . .

Three and a half years ago when I told Sophie that Rick died, she paused then said, "You know he used to say that you would probably outlive all of us."

I did kind of remember him saying that. Those words continue to reverberate through the echoes of my mind.

Riley

Where do I begin with Riley? She's the daughter of Rick and Ashley.

. . .

She experienced an inordinate amount of pain, stress, and feelings of hopelessness as a young girl. She says she doesn't remember much of what happened during her very early years. That might be a good thing. I can't imagine living through the hell that was a regular thing for her. If her mom and dad were partying somewhere, she might fall asleep late at night in a place she'd never been to before, among a cluster of other little kids she had never seen before. Sometimes the kids were locked in the basement while the adults gorked out upstairs.

Then in the morning, sudden fear. Where am I? Where's mommy? Where's daddy? I'm hungry. She would have to search through all the people passed out, till she found her parents.

She and her brothers were exiled to foster families five times from the time when she was two until she moved in permanently with Grandpa Joe at the age of ten. We rarely expressed emotions of any kind in the family I grew up in, so I can't wrap my head around all that happened to her in an ordinary day. I grew up with the same boring siblings, in the same boring house day after day, with parents who were always there, but rarely showed emotion. We were not affectionate. That's just the way it was.

Being the youngest of twelve kids, I understood rules and restrictions placed on us kids because I'd seen what happened to my older brothers and sisters when they got out of line. Of course if you asked them, they might tell you that I learned how to get by with stuff I shouldn't have done. And they'd probably be right. At least some of the times.

Riley did tell me that the one thing she remembers about her mom is that she got mad a lot. And mom frequently took it out on Hunter her twin brother, by yelling at him and hurting him. And her dad cried a lot. The few times Riley opened up about this she gave the appearance of getting anxious. She would hyperventilate, change positions, shake. So I seldom try to delve into it with her.

Something she doesn't seem to remember is how things were after Gunner was born. Rick and Ashley didn't come around much for a few years. I'm pretty sure I didn't see them at all while Ashley was pregnant with Gunner. In fact, he was four months old the first time I held him. What a cutie! He was a soft little roly-poly, just like his dad and uncle were at that age. I fell in love with him immediately. They started coming around a bit more for a while. Ashley didn't seem to be able to take care of Gunner. Riley took over on that responsibility. She always had his baby bag packed with plenty of bottles, his coat on. He was always clean and happy. She really was more like his mother than his sister in some ways. And she was five years old at the time.

* * *

(Riley kept a journal through much of her later teenage years. She made a copy of it for me earlier this year, and said she wanted me to include it in this book. Some of it was so heartbreaking, I couldn't stop crying as I read it. I asked her several times if she really wanted it in this book. She said she thought it might help keep someone from doing some of the stuff she did. Most of this is verbatim. Some things depicted may be fabricated in some cases to have it flow better, in other places to protect some people. As you'll see, it comes across without perfect grammar. Who does perfect grammar in their journal?)

Riley's journal

It was time for bed and I crawled in and lay down. Not a worry in the world. Just staying at grandma's house. I was ten years old and it was the weekend of Easter. Laying in my bed, I can't remember if I was asleep or not, but my grandma came in and when I looked up I saw her ... teary eyed ... And I wondered, is she crying?

She told me that my mom had died. I'm not sure if I said anything but I know I thought many things. And the first thing that came to my mind is, "Mom's not dead." I wondered why she would lie to me. She laid in the bed with me and we cried. But I still didn't want to believe it. And even years after that night, I still didn't believe it. I made up stories like my mom finally got away from all the "bad" people and she was with another family. I never grieved it. I would look her up on the internet, hoping one day I'd find her, and I never did. And I'm sure that's part of the reason I gave myself such a hard time growing up, giving everyone around me a hard time also.

I remember in fourth grade my teacher pulled me out of the classroom and asked me what's wrong? I told her my mom died. She actually ended up going to my mom's funeral. Everybody, all my family was at her funeral. Everyone was crying, but me. I was too scared to cry. To even see her casket. I didn't say good-by. I didn't believe it. Well I definitely blocked it all out of my mind. I didn't talk about it. My mom passed away when I was ten years old.

Riley experienced so much emotional pain as a youngster. And she did not know how to deal with it. How to release it from her inner self. She started cutting herself on her arms. It sounds like an odd thing when you first hear about it. It makes perfect sense to the person who has so much pain bottled up inside, and they don't have a way to express it. When she cut herself, Riley would feel high for a short time. The pain from the cut would release endorphins to help her body address the new pain and stress of the cut. That would last maybe a few minutes, and she'd think about cutting again. It was horrific to see all the scars on her forearms. At one point she told me she started cutting on her belly because it gave her a new sense of high that cutting her arms no longer provided.

Riley did talk about how the DARE (Drug Abuse Resistance Education) program that everybody went through in middle school impacted her. And it changed the direction of her life. The program was designed to educate children about drugs as a way to keep them from wanting to start using. It had the opposite effect on her. She knew her mom and dad used drugs. She knew her mom died of an accidental overdose. So, she wanted to try each drug that they used. And the DARE program gave her lots of insight. She wanted to feel what they felt when they used those drugs. And, she wanted to be with her mom.

Actually, any drug would do. She wanted to try them all. She had some friends who would help her out. They checked different medicine cabinets at other friends' houses. They found some interesting stuff. And tried a lot of it. She got hooked up with someone who got her started on weed. Riley had some with her on her way home from school one day. She was a bit leery of taking it home because she knew Grandpa would not approve. So she hid it in a ditch beside the road and planned to go back and get it later. Before later arrived, the police found the bag. It was easy for them to figure out who's it was — she had her name written on the bag — oh, and she was well-known to the cops by that time. As was her twin brother, Hunter.

One day some friends brought over some alcohol which she helped herself to, along with the little bit Joe had in his house. She and her friends were in Joe's back yard. Joe noticed her stumbling and bumping into trees on her way back to the house. Eventually she fell down. He thought she might have gotten a concussion, so he took her to Children's Hospital. She didn't have a concussion, but boy howdy, was she drunk. Her blood alcohol level was 214. Enough to kill her. I stayed with her so Joe could go home to sort things out and stay with the boys. Whew, she had some colorful language which she used a lot, and loud as she was sobering up.

At one point while she was in ER, she said she would kill herself if she had to go back home with Joe. That landed her an extra night in ICU. I stayed with her. She eventually calmed down and did return home.

She acted out with boys in school and at social events. She was banned from the local shopping mall for a year because she harassed a security guard. She snuck out at night to do, God only knows what. She became very disobedient and disruptive at home. One day she was at my house and asked to borrow my phone because she wanted check her Facebook page and her phone was dead. I let her use it, and didn't think another thing about it, after she went back home. The next few days, my phone lit up with her Facebook notifications. I tried to not read them. I really did try not to. But they were coming to my phone. It's hard to not catch a glimpse of what someone sends when you open it on your phone. Friday after work, I stopped by Joe's house. When Riley came out, I handed her my phone and told her to make it so I wouldn't get any of her Facebook stuff.

The expression on her face was priceless. Shock, fear, disbelief. Finally, she said, "That's impossible. They can't be going to you. What did you do?"

"Riley, I don't know how to get in your account. The only thing I can figure out is that you didn't turn it off when you were checking on things at my house last weekend. I've been getting fifty to a hundred posts a day."

Now there was just disbelief and fear left showing. I'm sure the things going through her head were questions about what some of those boys might have said, that she didn't want this grandma to read.

She said merely, "That's impossible."

"I don't know how it happened, and I don't want things that your friends want to say to you coming to my phone. By the way, Dakota wants to make out with you, but you think just one kiss would be enough to start with. And Dawson looks really hot with his shirt off."

Now there was nothing left but embarrassment showing on her face. She took my phone and asked, "Do you want me to close my Facebook account?"

I replied, "I think that Facebook can bring things into your life that can cause you pain and get you into trouble. But it's between you and Grandpa if you have an account." (I also knew she'd just open another account if she had to drop the current one. And besides Joe already checked the current account regularly.)

Eventually, by the time she was a sophomore in high school, she had been so out of control, she had to go to a partial hospitalization program. In this program, she would attend a school with other "out of control" kids. A big part of their day consisted of group counseling. The rest of the day, they kept up with their regular schoolwork. I think she liked not having so much schoolwork to do, and she got to rub elbows with other deviants her age. The thing she didn't like was not being able to spend time with the boys she liked to do stuff with.

She and Joe were very involved with children's services. Like it or not. Eventually it was determined that she would go a residential treatment center in Toledo. We could visit occasionally on weekends. She always looked good when we were there. She got in a lot of fights at first. The teachers and counselors there loved her spirit and reported they thought that once she got out, she would stay clean and be extraordinarily successful. Eventually the other girls there learned to leave her stuff alone. She actually made some friends there, too.

She worked her way through the program and nine months later, Joe and I picked her up and took her back home. She had so many plans for when she got home and talked nonstop the whole way. She was never going to use drugs again — now she realizes that no drugs are good for her. She sounded so confident that her life would be different. She wasn't even going to have sex till she was married. (Right.)

Having her return home was not my first choice. I didn't think Joe would be able to keep the boundaries she needed — I knew I wouldn't be able to do that. She would have access to her friends whom she did drugs with before. I was hoping she could go to a place that would help her transition slowly to independence. But no. Joe wanted her back home. He felt he could provide a better home life for her than anyone else could.

So, she was to do her schoolwork at home on her computer and do other things around his house the rest of the day. Well that worked for about a month. She reconnected with her former friends and schoolwork became less important. Then she hooked up with Pat, her new boyfriend. He was clean when they met. But that didn't last. Neither of them had jobs so they found a way to make money. Literally.

Joe was working at the Moose, a fraternal organization, when he got a call from the secret service. Yep THE secret service. They were at his house and wanted to search it. Joe told them to wait. His grandson was home alone, and Joe didn't want strangers in his house without him there. When he got there, black cars with darkened windows were near the driveway. Men with black suits, sunglasses, and earpieces standing nearby. The G-men followed Joe inside. They confiscated an odd-looking printer from Riley's room. Joe said he'd never seen it before. They took Joe's printer as well. Just because. Finally, they got to the garage. There they found some copy paper that was different from anything Joe had ever seen before. This confirmed what the secret service were sent to determine: Riley and Pat were making money. Literally. Not in Joe's house, exactly. They had made it somewhere else, then Pat told her to take the printer. So the means of making money was what they were looking for. The secret service had the equipment, but no evidence that Riley used it there at Joe's house. She got in trouble for it anyway.

I didn't see much of Riley after that. I got reports about her occasionally from Joe. She was on probation in different cities, different counties. Then she was on house arrest somewhere in a neighboring town. And finally, she and Pat took off for Florida. I was so worried about her. As it turned out my worst imaginations were nowhere near the terrible things she was experiencing.

Riley's journal (continued)

7/15

I've always thought about death. About suicide. I've many times throughout my life tried to commit suicide. I've failed many times. I said I didn't want to live to be 18. I didn't want to live to be an adult. I didn't want to live a long life. And I hated my life. When I turned 18 I met a guy and got on drugs. I'm 19 now and I'm clean. I've been 6 months clean and I still think about being 6 feet under. I in fact did live past 18. But I always have the choice to end my life.

And if ….

June 14, 2017

I just got released from jail in Florida. Before I got out, I contacted a family my boyfriend introduced me to. She said she'd pick me up from jail. And let me stay with them. When I got out of jail, I used their phone to try to contact her. Her phone was off. I called for hours. So I decided to walk to the gas station. Not knowing, I walked the wrong way. So I walked and walked. I literally walked the wrong way on the highway for miles. I didn't know where I was going or where I was at. It began to pour down rain. Cars would honk and stop. And ask if I needed a ride. I said no. I was drenched.

A black truck literally stopped in front of me on the highway. And says, "need a ride?" I was desperate. So, I hopped in. He asked me where I need to go. I say the nearest gas station. I explained my story. That I just got out of jail. And I needed to use a phone. As we pulled up to a racetrack, he asks me to pull my shirt up, and he'll take me to wherever I need to go. I got right out of the car. I walked inside and asked to use a phone. Her phone was still off. I began to lose hope. I walked outside and just cried. Standing in the rain.

An old man in a nice car said, "You alright?"

I shook my head "Yes."

But the truth was I was not getting anywhere. I was stuck and I knew that if I didn't get a ride I would never get anywhere. He asked me if I needed a ride. I got in his car. I was scared because I didn't know this man. Once again I explained my story, and I needed to get to Palm Coast. 45 minute drive. He said he'd take me and we started driving. He ended up taking me to his house where his mom lived with him. I made him drop me off at the nearest Greyhound and I called Nichole. She finally answered. I told her where I was at and she came on her way to get me. She was two or more hours away.

· · ·

My life before I was ten.

I was in many foster cares. Switching from my parents having custody to then foster care. I was in and out, being torn apart. But me and my twin brother stayed together. And five years after we were born, my brother Gunner was born. We always stayed together. When I was nine grandpa took on full custody of my brothers and my sister got adopted to another family. My dad has been MIA from our lives for a couple years by then. My mom would visit a lot. When I was ten, my mom died of a drug overdose.

And from the time me and my brothers were told, it was never talked about. I just lost my mom and I was too scared to cry at her funeral. I wanted to so bad for it not to be true. My twin grew and grew to be mean and hateful. And call me names.

When I was thirteen, I took a bottle of headache medicine hoping I would die. I just threw up. My twin would make fun of me and tell me he wished I would die, to go ahead and kill myself. He'd call me ugly. And anything you could imagine.

I grew up hating myself. Not long from that I started cutting myself. I went to a alternative school PHP in 8th grade. Honestly I wanted to die. The last day of 8th grade my twin was drinking and got me to drink too. All I remember was I couldn't stop downing bottles of who knows what. I woke up in the hospital. My alcohol level was .214 and from then on I was a mess. I went to school drunk, high off anything I could get my hands on. I took a handful of oxys and hoped it'd kill me and it didn't.

By then the law got involved and I was in and out of juvie. Running away when I was 14 or 15. My dad contacted me on Facebook and we soon got in in touch. And my dad lived in Kentucky. He got his legal and drug problems handled. He was being my dad but I couldn't get it.

My probation sent me to Toledo. For 9 months when I was 16. Me and my dad got close. He visited me every chance he could. I've been sexually abused by older men, people in foster care, and I was just scared. What if my dad did it too? And I just can't remember it. I was scared to get too close.

A few months after I got out of treatment my grandpa got a call on the phone. And they said my dad has been in an accident and we had come to the hospital. So we drove 2 hours. And when we got there I saw my dad in a room. He was dead. I was thinking ... my mom and now my dad ... I cried ... but I'd been through this once before. So I made sure I said good-by properly.

I didn't understand why god does these things ... take the people you love the most. I just did not get it. I hated god and I hated this world. What did I do to deserve this. But the truth is I didn't deserve the life I was given but god gave me this life because he knew I could handle it. After my dad died I came to believe that god took my parents so he could take me too. And I didn't want to live. Even past 18. So many times I tried taking pills and it just wasn't enough. Trips to hospitals and mental institutions. I just had a death wish. It was close to me turning 18 and the beginning of the new school year. I was going to the career center for electrical wiring.

I met this guy, Pat, at a friend who I moved in with. Me and this Pat actually started dating. And I soon moved in with him and his aunt within weeks of meeting him. At first we didn't use drugs. But I told him my goal was to try every drug even the needle. And I wanted to overdose. Just like my mom and die. So Pat got a drug (meth) and we used. And we used. And we used. And we sold it. And we lost our place to stay. We started doing illegal things to get money. We both got charges. Warrants.

So we left. To go to Florida. I was leaving my home. To another state. A month later, we got arrested and Pat went to prison. I was there because Pat and I bought a car and put his mom's name on the registration. That's what you do when you have a felony warrant against you in one state, and you need to get to another state, right? So, we took off from Ohio and drove to Florida. We might have gotten away with it except for driving straight through a toll booth. Without paying. What else could we do?

We had no cash. No credit cards. The highway patrol sent Pat's mom the ticket with a friendly reminder to pay the bill. No surprise, she was pissed. So, she told them what she figured we done.

. . .

We been in Florida about two months. Now we got another felony on our records. In Florida. The arrest was scary. We were stopped at a place off the road, minding our own business, when without warning, we were surrounded by six or seven police cars. Their doors opened. Every car had a cop standing by the open door with a gun pointed at us. Two of them had long guns. I was pulled out of the car by the meanest cop I ever saw. He threw me to the ground and told me don't move. I knew better than to challenge him on that. So, I laid there, spread eagle, face down on the road. I was too scared to cry, or even breathe. Pat warned me about Florida cops. They can get by with shooting a person if they just twitched a single muscle. Some of his friends tried it. They were shot. Dead. The cops got off with nothin each time. They can kill anybody, is what Pat told me. That's the law there. I was never so scared in my life as I was laying there on the road. It was almost a relief to complete the jail processing. I felt safer in jail than outside with the cops.

Pat was originally from Florida. He grew up kinda out of control. Got in trouble with the law when he was a kid. Got into drugs. Eventually started dealing coke and meth in Florida. That got him in trouble, so he went up to Ohio. To be with his mom, Sheila. Funny how that works. She went to Ohio to get away from him in the first place. Now he was clean and planned to stay that way. And he was back with her.

I started house hopping. Move in with one friend, stay a while, move on. I was free and I could do whatever I wanted. I wanted to be completely independent. Short tempered doesn't really express how quick my mood changed. I was more like a firecracker. I'd be fine one second then the next second explode. For no reason, really. So, I got pissed at one of the people who let me stay with them. I punched her in the gut. On purpose. Knowing she was pregnant. I wanted her to hurt. She hurt. And I ended up with a felony assault charge. Sheila let me stay with her after that.

Pat and I hit it off from the start. He wasn't using drugs at all at the time. He had a good job. He took care of me. We were good together. Then he decided to get some meth. I used meth for the first time with him. I liked it from then on. Damn what a feeling! Like I can do anything in the world. Like everybody loves me. Like I don't need anything else at all — no food, no drinks, no sleep. I felt so happy — happier than I ever felt before. I had more energy than I ever imagined. I was motivated to get up and do anything I wanted. I wasn't depressed. I felt great. It was unbelievable. I could go anywhere from eight hours to a couple days without eating or sleeping. Sometimes even longer. Like weeks. The bad thing is that it also made me feel paranoid. I hallucinated. I felt like people were always following me, and I didn't know what they wanted. I just knew I was scared and needed to keep moving.

I moved around house to house some more. Worked here and there. And then we took off for Florida.

· · ·

I got out on probation. For 9 months I tried to stay in Florida to be with Pat. I slept outside for months, behind stores, parking garages, tents in the woods. I was so miserable. I couldn't do it anymore. I called my grandpa and he got me a Greyhound ticket to Ohio. And I would turn myself into the police the day I got back.

When I got out of jail I really wanted to stay clean, but where I went there were people who used. I stayed clean for a short period of time and started using again. I was on probation. Every time I checked in she wouldn't drug test me so I kept using. It wasn't long before the people kicked me out. So I just started walking. Walking to my probation. When I got to my probation told her what happened, and she sent me to a domestic violence shelter. The girls there were mean and within a month I ended up taking all my prescribed meds at the same time and they took me to a mental hospital.

When I got out I was stuck downtown. And I didn't know nobody. I didn't know where to go so I just started walking. Days went by and I was still walking. I met people who were also homeless, who showed me good places to sleep at night. I hadn't showered in days. And I was almost 2 weeks clean from drugs. I was hungry. I was miserable. I was standing outside of a gas station asking people to use their phones. I needed to call my grandpa. I didn't know what else to do. A guy in a company truck pulled in. I asked to use his phone and told him I was stuck. My grandpa didn't answer. And what if he did? He's in Ohio. What could he do?

The man asked me to get in. He'll give a ride. I said no. But I gave in because he was persistent and I had no where to go. I was dirty and I was just so skinny. The guy took me to his house. He then asked me if I wanted to drink. I didn't want to drink at all. And I knew if I drank he was gonna be bad. He kept begging me. So I took a few shots. And before I knew it, I was blacking out. In and out. The man was on top on me and I just remember screaming, "Get off of me."

I woke up the next morning. And this man acted like nothing happened. He told me I could take a shower. And

I did. And I was confused. If what I remembered had happened. I'd been in a similar situation where I was raped and the guy acted like it didn't happen. So was this one of those times. No, because I know what happened.

He gave me some money and food and dropped me back off and said he'd be back after he got off work. A few hours went by and he had dropped me off at the beach. I walked literally 2 days before I realized he was never planning on coming back. I was of course at the beach and I hadn't ever been there before. I was scared. At night I would sleep on the beach. For about 3 weeks I just walked around asking for food. I literally lost myself. I was so hopeless, and I was miserable.

I called my probation and told him I was homeless, and I had nowhere to go. I asked him if I could get my probation changed to Ohio. I told him I had warrants and I didn't care. Jail was better than being homeless. I had talked to my grandfather and he said he get me a Greyhound. And I'd turn myself in. My P.O. told me I had to wait 4–6 weeks for it to get transferred. I waited about a month. And I told my grandpa it was transferred. It wasn't. But I was still hungry. Sleeping outside.

I came home the day before Christmas, and I turned myself in to the court the day after Christmas. I went from one county to another to the next. Then Florida put a holder on me. And Florida came and picked me up. The trip to Florida took 9 days. I left Springfield with 2 other girls. We stopped at jails in 6 different states. Dropping people off, picking new people up. Traveling in a paddy wagon with strangers, was no fun. We had to beg the drivers to stop so we could pee. Sometimes they would stop by the side of the road and watch us do our thing in the side ditch. And laugh. I got to Florida and they gave me 90 days and let me out of jail. I got on another greyhound and came straight back to Ohio. And waited for a bed at Women's Recovery Center.

My heart has lots of feelings / emotions. But it seems the little things get me more upset than the big ones. Like my parents dying, no big deal. But small stuff gets me more. Y?

May 11, 2018
Step one (worksheet)

1. How have chemicals placed your life and the lives of others in danger?

   I did some pretty dumb stuff. Stealing cars and running from police. Also taking my friends around dope boys. I could have been shot or killed.

2. How have you lost self-respect due to your chemical usage?

   I used around everyone. And didn't care who saw me, where I was at, and how I used. I also behaved in ways I never would have thought of if I was clean. It was just really embarrassing. I had no respect for myself. And it was degrading.

3. How has your chemical use affected your morals and values?

   When I was getting high I for some reason thought it was okay to rob people. As I got deeper in my addiction, I got worse and took robbing to the extreme. I would break into random peoples and steal anything and everything worth value. I guess because I was high. It was all about me and my high. And my morals changed rapidly.

4. What is it about your chemical use that those close to you object the most?

A lot of friends close to me objected to my needle use. They didn't like it. They'd rather me use without a needle. My family didn't really know I used. Or they just kind of was in denial. My brothers didn't like it because my mom died of drugs.

5. What changes in your attitude have you noticed or been told about?

   I'm not so emotional or bipolar. No one else has really told me what some of my changes are. But I have noticed some within myself.

6. How have you tried to control your consumption of alcohol or drugs?

   I have stayed 100% abstinent for just about 5 months. Really it has been pretty easy. I focused on myself. And stayed away from negative friends. I chose wisely where I went or what I did.

7. How many times have you tried to stop using chemicals?

   Many times. But this time I have put more effort and patience into "this time."

8. How have you tried to stop?

   I've tried to stop cold turkey. But at the same time, I was still living with my drug friends. So days, sometimes weeks, would go by I'd relapse and start again. I thought I could do it by myself and I could not.

9. What types of physical abuse has happened to you or others as a result of your use?

   I was very angry especially when I did not have drugs so I would lash out on my boyfriend at the time. Hitting him and screaming. I hurt the ones I loved the most. Visa versa.

10. What type of emotional abuse has happened to you or others as a result of your use?
    ?

16. Have you experienced blackouts or loss of memory.?
    Yes I have. I got really drunk one time. I blacked out and ended up in the hospital.

    Also, very much so with loss of memory.

17. What goals has your chemical use prevented you from achieving?
    I had goals … keeping a job, getting a job, graduating high school, electrician, getting an apt.

18. List three feelings you have tried to escape from by using chemicals.
    All of them.

19. Do you believe you are chemically dependent?
    Not anymore.

June 4, 2018
Tonight I got baptized. New me. I am forgiven. It feels good. Different. Just am very proud of myself. And I know that my mom and dad are and would be proud of me.
I love you mom and dad. I know I can do this.
I don't want to die anymore. I want to live for god!

Some thoughts from conversations with Riley

July 2018
Early this month I asked Riley if she would want to live with me instead of going back to grandpas. Next thing I knew, I was called in to interview for her to come to my house. I had written a letter to Riley including my rules: 1. No smoking at my house. 2. No friends over who have used drugs. 3. Get and keep a job.

During the meeting, we talked about smoking. I had already thought through that a bit more. I figured if she wasn't allowed to smoke on my property, she would walk the neighborhood smoking. I didn't want that. I suggested to her that even though she hadn't smoked for many months, she probably couldn't wait to have that first one. Her eyes got big, she nodded and agreed. I don't understand that need, but if that's what it took to keep her home, I'd accept her smoking — on the back patio only.

Riley also schooled me on friendships. She said she needs to be around people in recovery because people who haven't gone through it don't understand what she needs. That made sense. If she worked with people who want to go for a beer after work, or go out on weekends — camping, canoeing, etc., she would probably want to go with them. But if her friends were people who would help her when she doesn't think she needs to go to an AA or NA meeting; they would be there for her. They would be able to keep her sober. Well, that made sense, too.

And as far as getting a job, she wanted that more than anything. The biggest problem with this was finding a place that would accept someone with a felony.

So I passed the interview process. I went home and poured out all of my beer and alcohol. Some rum and whiskey had been up in my closet fifteen years. The unopened bottles I gave to Sophie.

After Riley was released from Women's Recovery, she moved in with me. Joe dropped her off at my house before I got off work. Riley had unpacked her stuff and settled into her bedroom — the same bedroom she lay in when I told her that her mom died. I sat down in the living room. She came out and sat on the couch. I think we were both a little nervous about what was happening. I wasn't sure what to talk about. Riley was bordering more on anxiety. Her legs were jumpy. She kept repositioning.

Since I like to have a plan for success, I asked her how she thought things would go; what would she need to do to stay successful in her recovery and be able to get out on her own. At the time I figured she would want to get her own place ASAP. I figured she could be out and on her own by Christmas, and we'd all be happy. She said her primary goal was to stay sober. She would go to ninety AA meetings in ninety days. She would get a sponsor. She would continue with counseling through The Community Network (TCN). She would do what she needed to do to complete her probation for her two misdemeanors and one felony. Dang. I felt like I didn't know her. I certainly didn't know what it would take for her to get through this. I have no idea what I said to her, but her response was, "Grandma, you don't get it. You have no idea what it's like to be an addict."

That was true. I had a lot to learn.

I asked her what kind of food she wanted. She didn't know what she wanted. I figured this would be an issue. Riley is a very picky eater. She always was. She claimed to be a vegetarian, but if she went to McDonalds, she would have a Big Mac because "they don't have any salads that taste good." Okaaay. I eventually came to be believe that she was not a vegetarian; she was a junk-food-etarian.

Since she couldn't tell me what she wanted to buy, we decided to go the store and she could pick out what she wanted. We got in the car and got about halfway to the store. It was very quiet. At the stop light I looked over at her and saw that she was crying. I asked what was wrong.

Riley said, "Grandma, I don't know if I can live with you. I never lived with you before. I don't feel comfortable with you." Her words came out in fits and starts, between her sobs.

I was speechless for a minute. Finally I said, "What do you want to do?" Pause.

"Do you want to go back and live with Grandpa?" Another pause.

"I think so."

"OK. That's fine. You can live where you want. If you want to live with Grandpa, he'd love to have you back."

Riley dried her tears, and looked over at me, "Really?"

At that point I didn't think going back to Joe's was a good idea. I feared that she would go back to her old ways, with her old friends because it would be so convenient. So routine. There's no bus route in that area, so she wouldn't be able to get anywhere on her own. I have a bus stop three blocks from my house. Yet I wanted her to know that her future is in her hands. She needs to make her own decisions.

I said, "Sure. Grandpa would love to have you stay with him. If you want, we can go home, pack up your stuff, and I'll take you there."

That calmed her down. "Ok."

She packed her stuff up again. Everything she owned fit in my car. She was ready to go.

I said, "It might be easier to get to an AA meeting before you go."

She agreed. I dropped her off at the meeting place. I waited for her in the parking lot when it was over. She got in my car, and said, "Grandma, I changed my mind. I want to stay with you."

I don't know what happened in that meeting, but I liked it. We went home and she unpacked and arranged things in her room. I called Joe to update him.

We drove to a lot of places the next day. The Job Center, the Medicaid place, a couple of places that we heard might hire someone in her situation. I thought it was frustrating. Riley held it all together. She was calm, conversant. We stopped at Wendy's for a late lunch. I got a salad, you know, to go with her flow. She got a ginormous hamburger and basically inhaled it. She kept saying that she thought there was a place called Youth Build. It was a program for young adults who were in a situation like her. In trouble with the law. Didn't graduate high school. We couldn't find it. We went back to the Job Center and asked them about it. Well, what do you know? That's where it was. They were starting a new class and would have signups the next day!

That evening, back home, and Riley again said she'd rather live with Joe. OK. She started packing her stuff up. This time she went to a meeting before we put it in my car. After the meeting, she said she changed her mind and wanted to stay with me. Such turmoil for her.

We walked in the Youth Build classroom at the designated time the next morning. Someone called out my name several times. I was sure I didn't know anyone there, so it couldn't have been me they were talking to. Finally I looked in the direction of the sound. My oldest nephew's daughter was calling to me! What tha? Sandy was the director of the program. What a relief to have someone in my family here! This would work, I was convinced.

We watched a film about the program and listened to the presentations. Wow! This was just what Riley needed. She would actually get paid when she completed each section of her GED. She would be trained in construction and get certified in different aspects. It was awesome.

She took the bus every day to the training place which was way past the other side of town. Fortunately, the bus that stopped near me would take her to within three blocks of where she needed to be. Youth Build provided her bus passes. I so admired her determination to get through the program and qualify for a good job. She was so refreshing to have in my home. I loved it. I told people it was like having an angel in my home. She glowed with inner peace, love, and happiness. It reminded me of the heavenly glow I saw in nuns when I was a kid.

She got a job at Wendy's within a couple weeks. It was close to home. She could walk to it. She had an impossible schedule. Leave for Youth Build at seven AM. Get to counseling by three Monday, Wednesday, Friday. Get to meetings every day. Get to three different POs for her legal issues monthly. Go to Wendy's about seven on days she didn't have counseling. Work till close. She did community service at a Goodwill store on Saturdays. Something had to give. She eventually quit at Wendy's.

My home life was different from what it had been before Riley moved in. She liked to watch *Orange is the new Black*. I learned a lot about prison life that I probably didn't need to know as we sat and watched it. I also learned about addiction from Riley as the weeks went on. I met a lot of her friends, as I would visit with them on the patio when they came over. On Fridays Riley and I would sit on the patio and play cards. She knew lots of games. She smoked cigarettes. I occasionally had a cigar. We drank water. Her twin brother, Hunter, and his friends came over sometimes. My new normal was nowhere near normal from my perspective.

It was not easy for us to settle in together at first. I had lived alone for more than ten years. She had never lived long term with me. We did settle in and shortly after had a good relationship.

. . .

We had lots of talks about things she'd experienced. It was shocking. After she lived with me for several months, Riley said she wanted me to help her write her book. She wants a book to describe what she thought and felt when she was out of control. She wants people to know. I tried to write about it from her perspective. So I wrote. I wrote about our conversation when she called on the day of her twin brother's high school graduation. With subsequent conversations with Riley, I had a better idea of where she was and who she was that day.

. . .

This is what I imagined she was living as she filled in some of the blanks:

> Damn I thought as I slammed down the receiver on the black wall phone in the visiting room outside the pod I had to stay in with the other prisoners. I wanted to scream at the top of my lungs, but that would just draw attention from the other prisoners I had to live with in this hell hole. I didn't want any attention from anybody in here. I just

wanted to run – as fast and as far as I could to get away from this jail. But that wasn't going to happen, because I couldn't even get out of this room without a guard letting me pass by.

I just got off the phone with Grandma Nancy. It was so good to hear her voice. I cried at first. That's all I could do. Just sobs with spurts of words gushing through my mouth in single syllables. I told her where I was. Jail in Orange County, Florida.

Getting back to my phone call, Grandma said she was on her way home from my twin brother's (Hunter) high school graduation ceremony back in Ohio. Damn, I thought. Hunter graduated today. I could have been there with him. If I hadn't done some really stupid shit, that got me arrested so often. If people would have just helped me, given me what I needed I wouldn't be in this place. Now I just want to be home. I want to be with people who I love and who love me. I want to be with my family.

Grandma asked me if I was getting drugs in jail.

"No Grandma, I can't get drugs in jail."

"Do you miss the drugs you generally used, since you can't get them there?"

"No Grandma, I don't miss them."

"Well then, Riley, maybe when you get out, you should stay away from people who use drugs."

"Grandma, have you ever been an addict?"

"No Riley, I haven't."

"Then you have no idea what it's like. It's really hard to be an addict because you know that the thing you need is the thing that's going to kill you."

I added, "Addicts are generally good people and they help other addicts out when they can. They are just not real reliable."

Grandma laughed at that. It felt good to hear her laughter. I laughed, too. Probably the first time I laughed in this hell hole.

After we hung up, I felt so empty. So pissed. So lost. How can I be sitting in this jail? Today was supposed to be my high school graduation, too. Why did I drop out of high school? I'm only eighteen. All my life, I blamed everybody else for my feelings. I blamed everybody else for my failures. And I guess I lived up to my failures. And created more.

I was a firecracker at first in this jail. Just like I was in Ohio. I'd be really sweet, then get jacked up for no reason and want to beat on someone. Never been in adult jail before. Been in juvie many times. In juvie you have your own cell. With a toilet. Your supplied a jump suit, underwear, bra. You have little to no interaction with anyone. Your in your cell most of the day.

Adult jail is different. Your in a big room/dorm/pod with thirty to sixty other people. You eat together, sleep together, breathe together. There is no privacy. If you get with some real bitches, your screwed.

I even got jumped in there. I probably asked for it. All I wanted to do right then was sleep. All day. All night. And then all day, and all night again. I wanted my light off. My bunk mate came in all loud and pissy and turned it back on. I got up and turned it off. When she turned it back on, I jumped off my bed and started yelling. A lot of other people didn't like me yelling, so they came in and five or six started beating on me. I thought they would kill me. I was on the ground crying. The CO came in and pulled them off me. I sat in a one-man cell for a few days. Then they moved me to a different pod. I learned really quick to keep quiet and keep to myself. And I did just that. I did make some friends. I played spades with them. It felt like

I was in there for months. Every day went by slow. When I came in, I was under weight. I weighed 108 pounds. I'm usually 135 – 140. I was skinny.

Looking back, it wasn't a good idea for me to cut off the ankle bracelet I was wearing — I was on house arrest in Springboro, Ohio. For punching that pregnant girl in the gut. It was a good thing for me when I happened to be in jail in Dayton and I met the granddaughter of a very rich, well known doctor. We became friends, and her family talked my PO into letting me stay at their house during my house arrest. Score! They had a mansion. With a pool. I could do anything I wanted. Except leave the property.

I got hooked up with Pat again. Thank God. I needed to break outta there. Living rich is nice. Just not for me. I needed to be free to go where I wanted. We planned my escape. We knew I had to get out because I got a warrant for my arrest in the mail. Maybe it wasn't such a good idea to let Pat talk me into helping him making counterfeit money. And keep the evidence at Grandpa Joe's. Pat wanted me to have the printer at my house cuz the cops were gittin close to findin out. I'm so glad we never actually printed any off at grandpas.

It took a while, but somehow, I cut through the ankle bracelet. I don't know what those things are made of but, with a lot of effort a scissors will cut through them. I threw it in the corner of my bedroom, and away we went.

Even though I had been to juvenile detention when I was a kid, I never thought I'd be in adult jail. In another state. Dang. I thought about everything I did and how silly, no stupid, it all was. What drugs made me become. I was pissed at Pat for dragging me into this. But I was also scared. I'd never been to adult jail. It was so different from juvie.

I look around the pod I'm in – probably fifty to sixty girls. There were seven or eight more pods that size. These women are mean. A lot of them looked like they belonged there. I learned quick from living in a world like this, nobody belongs here. They were just surviving – living the only way they knew how. Many of them had no teeth. They were all banged up. They'd been out there. Going hard. A lot of them there were homeless. Like I'd been.

All the times I been in juvie, drugs weren't available. Same with this grown up jail. Once in a blue moon someone would bring in drugs here when they would book in. But that was rare. So being it jail was a time for everyone to get sober.

Nobody wanted to be in there. But it was like a safe haven. Nobody had to worry about where they was gonna sleep. How they was gonna get food to eat. Or how they was gonna pay for any of it. It was all given to them – free. A place you don't have to worry about any of that. Of course, there were people in there who weren't addicts or alcoholics. But they wouldn't stay long. And they'd probably never come back.

There's this emptiness us addicts need to fill. And for a long time, drugs filled that spot for me. After being on them for so long, it don't work no more. For some it works for years. For others it doesn't work very long at all. Everybody – addicts or not – we all want to feel good. We do things that makes us feel good. Drugs and alcohol was that for me for a long time.

How the hell did I get here?

After she read it, she looked at me and asked, "How did you do that, Grandma?

"Do what?"

"Get in my head and write what I wanted to say?"

Of course, when she read it, I had a lot of F-bombs included, as that's the way I figured a person who'd been I jail would talk. She never cussed the whole time she was with me. She was always polite and respectful and continues to be that. Interestingly, when I told her I took out the cussing, she voiced upset. That's who she was then. She wants it to be real. I'm still debating ….

Living with Riley

September 2018.
Within months, Riley got through the first phase of the Youth Build program. She had to get on a different bus to get to work. That meant she had to walk twice as far to get to the bus stop. It was endearing to watch her head out down the driveway. Her lunch bag, her purse, and her safety helmet on her head. I got to where I really trusted her. I decided to let her use my truck. I love my truck. But it just sat there. So ….

In short order she figured out that having a truck while most of her friends had no vehicle caused problems. Her friends kept bumming rides from her. She loved being able to drive; she didn't like being taken advantage of. People wanted to get places, but they had no gas money for her. She was getting used to her new norm — having something legal others wanted from her. And being taken advantage of so they can get it.

During this time, Riley was getting connected with former friends. One couple came over with their toddler who was in diapers. They were getting Medicaid benefits and hoping to have two or three more kids. I asked them how they could afford to have more kids. They just stared back at me with puzzled looks on their faces … for God sake they had Medicaid and had the right to have as many kids as they wanted. That was the American dream. I was sure they hadn't considered that they would have to cover expenses for their kids. I couldn't stand it and went in the house.

Another of her friends, Cassidy, lost custody of her four-year-old to her mom. She felt cheated; she would be a good mom.

She got pregnant three more times. Each pregnancy ended in miscarriage. I think she's the one who got Riley some pot ten days before Christmas. Wouldn't you know, Riley had to meet with her PO the next day and had to drop urine. It tested positive for fentanyl. She went directly to jail.

· · ·

I am positive that Riley never had a wonderful Christmas. Churches provided gifts for some of the Christmases when her parents were together. Rick and Ashely learned how to appeal to churches at Christmas time. The kids got loads of presents from anonymous church goers who felt like they were doing a Christian act by helping out the downtrodden. That was an eye opener for me. And shocking. What tha! I wanted to shake some sense into Rick. How could my son pull off such a scam??

And then her mom died. How can a child enjoy Christmas without her mom?

This one was no exception. She sat in jail over Christmas. And then over New Years. She worked in the kitchen at the jail so she could have more visits from friends. One visitation was with Sophie and her five-year-old daughter, Megan.

Megan is a piece of work. She asked Riley on a visit around Halloween, "What's the scariest bee in the world?"

"I don't know, What?"

"A BOO Bee!"

Riley nearly fell off her seat, laughing. Megan wasn't sure it was even funny. I'm sure she does not know to this day that telling that joke made Riley feel more normal. Geez, her five-year-old cousin told her a joke like as if it was the most normal thing in the world. Megan accepted Riley. And Riley felt like she continued to have a place in our family. Even if she was in jail.

I went to court for each of her hearings over the holidays. It was weird to see my baby girl walk in the room and sit in the prisoners' box in her black and white striped jail costume. She didn't look at me — not even a glance. (I later found out that prisoners are instructed not to look at the gallery or show any emotion. If they did, they would been given extra time in jail.) The judge was bad ass. He made her stay longer than we originally anticipated. Her public defender seemed kind of flakey. I wondered if she ever got anyone off early. Without the maximum jail time.

I wrote the judge a letter highlighting the rules and restrictions Riley would have if he released her back to me. Six people from Youth Build had also written letters to the judge outlining her character, and work ethic. We were all there in the courtroom. It was mid-January by this time.

The public defender pleaded for Riley to be allowed to return home. She did a surprisingly good job. The judge took his time. He had our letters on his desk. He reviewed mine out loud. He took his time some more. It seemed hard for him to say what he was about to say. Finally, he said he was impressed with the letters, and our commitment to help Riley. But she had all this support before, and she used drugs anyway. What's to keep her from using again? Then he added that things might not be so bad if she hadn't used fentanyl. She could have died. My hopes were sinking. I was feeling myself collapsing into my lap. Then he said he will give her one more try. But if she ever is back in his court, she will be in jail a long time. He let her out.

Joe dropped her off at my place that afternoon. Once here, she apologized for what she did but added that she didn't know the weed was laced with anything. She promised to stay off everything and stay away from people who use. She seemed serious. I reiterated that I will not have someone living with me who uses drugs.

$\bullet$ $\bullet$ $\bullet$

Riley had been begging for a dog. By mid-March I came to believe that a dog would be good for her. I felt she would be responsible for the dog's care. We looked at puppies at SICSA for weeks. Finally, she picked one out. It was mostly black with white on her chest. Short hair with a little fluffiness behind her ears. And a couple long hairs at the tip of her tail. We were told that "Cinderella" was one of eight pups in a litter and had to be resuscitated at birth. They expected her to have some neurologic problems but could not guess how they would be manifested. The worker asked Riley how she would deal with a dog that maybe couldn't walk or had other issues.

She responded, "I'll just love her more."

She brought the puppy home and renamed her Piper. As it turns out Piper is also the name of the main character in *Orange is the new Black*.

Piper did show some neurologic issues after a few weeks. She held her right hind leg up as if it was paralyzed when she ran. When we noticed it, I said she's got to run a lot and use that leg. Riley wanted to lay with her on the couch; I took Piper running. Riley wanted a lap dog no matter how big she got. I wanted a dog to run and play with in the back yard. Piper runs like a thoroughbred quarter horse now. Unfortunately, she can't hear. She's not much of a guard dog.

THE DISAPPEARING BEGINS

In about 2012, I started noticing that Josh had the smell of beer on his breath, every time I was near him. It didn't matter if it was evening, afternoon, or morning. He always smelled of beer and cigarettes. Within months after I noticed that, I also noticed that he was losing weight. I made sure I hugged him close every time I was near him. For one reason, I wanted to prove myself wrong. Also, I just somehow knew he was disappearing because he was drinking so much. His ribs became more and more prominent in his back. His back felt like an old washboard when I hugged him and moved my fingertips over the ribs in his back.

Some other things started showing up. His fingers trembled. It wasn't really shaking like people with Parkinson's. It was like each separate finger trembled independently from the rest. Ever so slightly. Not his wrist. Not his whole hand. Just his fingers. His penmanship got worse with time.

This went on for years, all the while the trembling becoming more and more noticeable. When I was on my way home from my brother, Alphonse's, funeral I got a call from Joe. Josh was in the hospital. He drove himself there because of severe abdominal pain. Crap, I thought. This can't be good.

I changed course and went to the hospital to see what was going on. I got to his room and a bit anxiously walked in. Double crap. His IV was a banana bag. I'd seen that many times over the years. It has an unmistakable yellow color like a ripe banana because of the vitamins and minerals in it. It's given to people who have nutritional imbalances. In this case, alcoholism.

My chest felt heavy. I chatted with Josh for a bit as he lay there looking sheepish and innocent. His pain had lessened with the meds he got. He was joking around as if nothing was going on. I'm sure he wanted a cigarette. And some beers. It had been hours since he had anything. I asked the nurses about his liver function test results. They were all high. The one that stood out was Lipase at 1200. Normal range is about 23 – 85. I'd never heard of one that high before this.

That was about all I could handle that day. My brother's funeral. Now a better understanding of just how sick Josh was. At six—five, his usual weight was 220. He looked good at that weight. Now he was 160! Nothing but skin and bones, really. Audrey had told me that Josh wasn't eating much. If he put a little helping of food on his plate, it would disappear. Most of went under the table where their dog, Lassie sat in wait. Lassie was huge by this time. And Josh was skinny.

The next day, I had to go to ICU to see him. The epiphany of where he was medically, and what he was going through was ever more frightening. Day by excruciatingly painful day. Audrey and I took turns staying overnight with him over the next several days. She sometimes would lie in bed with him and talk about how he would get better and things would be even better in their family once he stopped drinking and smoking. He was calm and happy with her lying next to him. And he agreed to everything she planned for them.

The DTs were beginning about day three. He was anxious, with exaggerated jerking of his arms and legs. Talking nonsense, wanting to get dressed and go to work. When no one would get him his clothes, he got even more anxious and angry. His vital signs were impossible to maintain. Blood pressure as high as 220/100, pulse 153, respirations 24. It was agonizing to watch him. He said some things to me that were so uncharacteristic. Threats. Lies. Just plain meanness. So strange coming out of his mouth. To top it off he was tied to the bed — both wrists, both ankles, and a chest restraint. It seemed like he was being tortured, quite frankly. I hated it.

After three days of watching this I could not understand why the doctor allowed it to continue. I agreed with a nurse who shook his head and said, with a very concerned expression on his face, that Josh couldn't go on like this much longer. So he was given meds to make him sleep, let his body rest. Of course, he wouldn't be able to breathe on his own with all these meds, so he was put on a vent. Triple crap. A mother should never have to see her child on a vent. Under any circumstances.

Four days of watching a machine breathe for him, and it would soon be time to make a decision. That's about the longest a person is kept on a vent. And so it was. The doctor asked me to leave the room as they pulled out the endotracheal tube. I did. When I was called back in, he looked so different. I could see his entire face with no tape, no machines attached. He was so handsome. And he was breathing on his own!

By this time test results showed that his gallbladder was less efficient, half his pancreas was not functioning (He would be diabetic for the rest of his life.), his liver was much less effective, and he had two blood clots in his lungs. Then to top it off, his kidneys shut down and he needed dialysis. All that damage. But he was alive, breathing on his own and could recover. He was transferred to a subacute hospital setting, where he received dialysis treatments for three more weeks. He was in the hospitals for a total of seven weeks. He still wasn't eating. He still was skinny. But his lab results looked good.

Before he went home, I asked him what he thought his problem was. He didn't pause before he responded, "I'm an alcoholic."

I asked what he needed to do to get better.

Again, without a pause, "No more drinking or smoking."

I thought, "Wow, that was easy." I really didn't think he would be able to say those words for a long time to come. Words come easy. Recovery does not.

◦ ◦ ◦

He was home for two weeks and wanted to get back to work. But he was weak, too weak to work. While a home health care nurse was there, he vomited a lot of blood and had a seizure in the kitchen. EMTs took him back to the emergency room. Not much going on there. So he went home again.

Over the next two months he had seizures, and more vomiting of blood. Eventually, a few months later, he ended up at a different hospital. And on a vent again. And in four-point restraints again. Standing by his side all I could think of was, "How much more can he take?" And, "Dang he's handsome."

Somehow, he was able to pull his breathing tube out. I guess he didn't really need it after all. His sense of humor was intact. He was so funny lying there in bed looking sheepish, and guilty. He explained to me and Audrey how he pulled out the tube, and we should be proud of him for figuring it out, especially since he was anesthetized and tied hands and feet to the bed. It was hard to not laugh as he tried to get sympathy from us.

Again, I heard a doctor tell Josh he was very sick, and he dare not have even one more beer, or smoke one more cigarette.

Again, I asked Josh if he knew what was wrong with him. Again, he said he was an alcoholic and would never drink or smoke again. Although he was no more believable than the last time, it felt good to hear him say those words.

When I picked him up from the hospital a week or so later, he said very angrily and determinedly, "I'm never coming back here again."

I felt queasy as he said it. I wanted to know what he meant by the statement. Did he mean he was going to take control of his life, and not pick up another drink or cigarette? Or maybe he meant that no matter what, he was going to continue drinking and smoking till it killed him, but he wasn't going to be hospitalized there again. Sadly, I reasoned, the latter was the more probable.

So many times in the past, with Rick I tried to get to the bottom of what he might be thinking. I asked questions and tried to delve into his mind, make him believe my way was better than his. Doing that seemed to put a wedge between us. His reality, thought process, logic was way past anything that I could understand. So I stopped asking what was going on. Everything he said was a lie anyway. The same was holding true for Josh. It had become easier for him to lie than to tell the truth, even if the lie was inconsequential.

This reminds me of way back when the boys were in high school, and Joe and I were eating dinner with a couple at a church function. The other couple laughed heartily when we expressed some concerns about things Rick was doing, and then lying about it. They said simply, "We could always tell when our teenagers were lying ... their lips were moving!" That made sense to me. And seemed to apply to both of my sons.

• • •

After Rick died in May 2016, I wanted to have Sophie and Josh come over and the three of us deal with our grief together by sharing stories about Rick. I wanted to have my shrinking family close to me. I wanted to savor any words they said. I wanted to hear their memories of things my three kids did together. I wanted to hear happy stories. I wanted to share my grief as a way to get through this tragedy. Sophie came over and seemed glad to be part of this. Josh, however, didn't show. Instead, Audrey came. That was confusing. I'm always glad to see her but it was disappointing to not have Josh there. The conversation just wasn't what I felt I needed that day. Yet it was healing.

Josh seemed sullen, even more detached from me as time went on. Not so much like an actively grieving brother. Just kind of empty. In some ways it seemed like it was no big deal to him. He went on with his life. They hadn't been all that close in recent years anyway. Josh had a chip on his shoulder and not even the death of his brother could knock it off. It was painful to see he couldn't forgive his brother for ... something. I didn't know what. One day, a few months later, when I was just kind of done with his sour disposition, I asked him if his brother was calling him home.

Ooo, that struck a chord, or at least his expression changed. He looked me in the eye, said, "No."

Then looked away and left my house. That was weird.

Josh continued to keep his feelings about Rick's passing to himself, or at least he didn't share any thoughts with me. I was never sure if he was even mourning at all. Then later that year, around Thanksgiving, we decided to put Rick's ashes in the same cemetery niche as his wife's ashes are in. Joe, Rick's three kids, Sophie, Josh and I were there on yet another sad day for our family. Another milestone to process.

Josh put himself in charge of keeping the candle lit. It couldn't stay lit. It was a cold, windy, rainy afternoon. No flame could stay lit under the circumstances. I started off with a prayer, and the purpose of our gathering. It was again heart retching. There we were saying good-by to Rick. Again. We all had a turn at talking about what Rick meant to us. By this time Riley was already in the car, her short fuse could not handle any more, even if she was maybe a little stoned. Joe was distraught — he talked about some of the good times. Gunner literally backed up, out of the group.

Sophie said she wasn't going to lie; Rick had done some bad things to her and she forgave him for everything. She just wished she had gotten to know him better when he came back to our family. She wished she could have known who he was.

Josh openly wept; he could not speak.

Hunter sad, "My life changed when I moved in with Dad. I don't know who I'd be without …" What a tearjerker. He couldn't continue.

Josh continued to look frazzled, empty, confused even as we went to dinner afterward. I thought, "Well maybe now it hit him, having been at the cemetery. Maybe now he would be able to quit drinking."

He just kept travelling down the disappearing path.

WE'RE NOT IN KANSAS ANYMORE

Memorial Day weekend 2019 started out being just another ordinary weekend. I can't say I even remember the first ninety-nine percent of it. Probably went out to eat. Might have played golf. Sat outside and enjoyed the wind and rain late that Monday. Not a bad evening storm. Just some lightening, thunder, wind. A nice spring storm.

Then I went inside to get ready for bed. I turned on the TV to watch the news. Holy crap! All the local stations had emergency weather notifications on instead of regular programing. Crap, it looked like a tornado just went through Joe's neighborhood! I hesitated a nano second. Then called him. His voice was loud, not at all calm. He stuttered as he spoke. It was more like a deep pain and distraction. He said the roof was blown off his house.

No need to say any more. "I'll be right there." I said.

Hunter and his girlfriend, Kirstin, came in right then with two massive dogs — their white husky and some big ole dog they were taking care of. Everybody was excited. Riley came up from the basement to see what all the commotion was about. I had just figured out that another tornado looked to be heading down Joe's throat. I called him back and said I'd be a while. There was another one heading toward him. Take cover.

Hunter was getting more and more agitated about the whole situation. He was insistent on saving his grandpa, brother and uncle from sudden death. Or worse.

I did my best to stop him. I said, "Don't you dare drive into a tornado. Just wait a couple minutes till this one passes."

Bam! He and Riley took off in his ram-shackled rattletrap of a car. Pissed me off. Nothing I could do. They were gone and I hoped they would not get blown deep into the land of Oz.

I continued to watch the emergency on TV all the while knowing my family was *in* the emergency. Finally, as I was putting on my shoes, it looked like the storm was a few blocks past Joe's house. I sat Kirstin on my bed, along with four dogs, eyes wide open, tails wagging, on high alert. None of the dogs were bothering another. They all seemed to know something was going on and they wanted to do … whatever. I told Kirstin I was going out to see what I could do. She seemed frightened, not so sure she wanted to stay at my house with no one else there — just dogs. I told her to keep watching TV and let me know if, yet another storm is coming, or if she hears from someone else. I considered her command central. I was glad she was there. I needed someone to monitor the situation for us.

I took off. In search of, I didn't know what.

I was met with the first of many shocks, that seemed to occur almost instantaneously. Joe's house is about eight miles from mine. I was within two miles and was about to turn onto the main street that would take me to his street. I couldn't turn onto that street. There were trees and parts of houses covering that road six to ten feet high. Clearly, I couldn't go that way. The police directed me to keep going. No worries. I know this neighborhood like the back of my hand. I used to run there, three to six miles several times a week when I was young, buff, and lived in an adjacent neighborhood.

My eyes were bigger than saucers. More like dinner plates, as I took in the destruction in this normally calm, quiet neighborhood. More and more branches and parts of houses on the streets, on the yards, everywhere. I could see through apartment buildings, and houses as I slowly drove over big branches, and tried to avoid roofs, walls and other debris from homes that might have nails in that could flatten my tires, without giving a second thought to what my purpose in life was right then. I just had to keep moving.

Lightening was off to the east, followed by the softer grumbling of thunder as the storm was losing its power; its decibel level receding slowly to zero. Just a light rain coming down from the heavens. At times the clouds looked angry. Other times they moved apart to allow stars to shine through. (Singa, singa.)

I came upon two people cautiously, lumbering toward me. Looking like zombies. They were also just experiencing the shock and taking in what now looked like a war zone. The peoples' eyes. OMG. Empty fear, disbelief besought with the realization that maybe, just maybe, they had outlived the horror of the storm. And might be safe. I rolled down my window and asked how bad their home was. Geez. Their house had not been hit. It seemed to be totally intact. They were walking across the street to see what was happening with their neighbor, whose house I could see through. We seemed to be stuck in the night of the living dead.

I eventually meandered back to the main road. It was clear for several hundred feet, but I could not go down Joe's street. It was totally covered with debris.

I heard from Joe or Hunter or Riley or Josh, I don't remember who. They were safe and heading back to my place. I turned the car around and went back the same way I came. There was no other way to go. Every street was covered with debris from houses, branches, entire trees. The unmitigated definition of the neighborhood changed because of that storm in just a matter of minutes. No longer was it a close-knit community of people who had lived next to each other year after year, celebrating all the milestones of raising their kids together. All that connectedness had ruptured and was bleeding out into the streets as neighbors tried to reconnect with people they loved; some who lost everything they owned, some who lost nothing but a few hours of sleep. Each of them experiencing an emptiness and horror they had never before known. Each person seeking hope that the morning would come, and all this would prove to be a terrible nightmare. It was not to be.

My family was finally safe in my house. I did a brief visual exam of each person. They were each shaken by their own experience as evidenced by some kind of inexplicable tension that their bodies and minds wouldn't allow to escape. And yet they were relieved to be in a safe place. No one was badly bruised, swollen, bleeding or crying in pain. And no one was boisterous, euphoric or exulting. There was a general sense of relief that we were all safe.

Once I realized that, I took Riley and Hunter off to the side individually and lit into them. "Don't you ever drive into a place about to be hit by a tornado again. You could have been killed. Or worse."

I paused, hugged them, and said, "Thanks for getting everyone here safe."

. . .

Then the stories began to erupt. The emotional pressure had to come out. They had each looked death in the eye, in a different room, under one roof that blew away into the night. You can't hold that in without exploding.

Joe and Josh had been standing outside watching the lightening show. It was past 10:30 and dark. They could only see the roiling of the clouds when their world was lit up by lightening. The clouds were heavy with water, just waiting to be sliced apart and a tsunami of water unleashed on the earth below. Finally, when the thunder shook them to their bones at the same instant that the lightening made their hair stand straight out on their arms, they decided to head inside the house. Joe made it to the kitchen. Josh was still standing in the front room when the storm's wrath cut loose. The front window was open about a foot to allow for pressure changes. The wind blew in with such a vengeance that he was picked up and thrown against the kitchen wall then hallway wall. He was knocked unconscious. Joe was partially safe from falling debris as he was standing next to the refrigerator. A couple of big pieces of something hit his shoulder, but the fridge stopped the bulk of the ceiling and roof from crushing him. He doesn't think he was knocked out, but I kind of wondered. It seemed like there was a lapse of time in his story.

Gunner's story was unbelievable. He was lying in bed and realized he couldn't move his legs. He looked up and saw that the ceiling was on top of them. He texted Joe, "Help me." Then covered his head and in an instant couldn't move his upper body. He shoved that debris off him, and as he looked up he saw the lightening and felt the rain pelting down on him in buckets. Not only was the ceiling gone, so was the roof. He shouted out every obscenity he ever heard as loud as he could, to no avail. The rage of the storm pulverized his tiny voice to where he couldn't even hear himself scream. He found his boots, put them on and went in search of the others. The walls of the hallway were holding up most of the roof above them. Josh was dazed but had gotten out from under the bulk of what had fallen and was sitting on it. Joe was in the front room in similar shape.

It was about then that I called him again and told him another storm was coming and to take cover. Then three of them went into the new bathroom. And awaited their fate. Shortly, the second horrific storm passed, and Hunter and Riley were there to the rescue. I'll bet they were a sight — five adults and a big dog in a car could fit four people snugly.

So, I had seven adults and five dogs in my house at a little past midnight that night. The storms were past. We could all pretty much breathe a sigh of relief. Hunter and his entourage — Kirstin and two large dogs — went home.

Josh seemed the most disheveled. His tall, lanky body. His clothes wrinkled and still drying. His hair which is normally short and well coifed, had about two inches of insulation fibers in it. He didn't want to, but I made him take a shower. I didn't want to even think about the toxins he was carrying around on his head and clothes.

Eventually everybody's adrenalin had worn off. It was the middle of the night and we were all ready to get some shut eye. Hunter and Kirstin went home. Riley and Gunner went in the basement to sleep. Joe took over the guest room that Riley had been using. Josh got out the air mattress and slept in the office. Everybody was safe. I went in my room and quickly fell asleep. How? I don't know. But I slept like a rock.

· · ·

The next morning there was a tension in the air that we all felt. True, we were all safe. But what comes next? I felt like we could make things work. We had to. That's what we always do, right?

First off, nobody wanted to eat breakfast. That was kind of a relief to me because I didn't really want to make breakfast for everybody. Josh, Joe and Gunner took off to see what their house looked like. I followed closely behind. The main street to get out to their house was kind of cleared off already. It was passable, at least. There was no chance of getting down their little street. Along the way apartment buildings had some units with only shower stalls and toilets still intact. Walls and roofs were gone. Just studs and sky visible. Then in the same building, other units were totally intact. So incredibly odd.

We had to take a back way to get to where Hunter had parked in a playground near Joe's house. We parked in an apartment lot and walked through the woods to get to Hunter's truck. My gawd. The entire neighborhood looked like a ground zero where a bomb had exploded. It would take months to clean it up. Leaves were stripped off trees. Not one tree had all its branches. Most trees had been uprooted and tossed about like pick up sticks. The houses were in similar condition to the apartments two miles away.

It took my breath away to see Joe's house. The roof on the old part was gone. The doors and windows were intact. Insulation everywhere inside. The ceiling in Joe's bedroom was on his bed. It was just weird to stand in the front room and see nothing but sky up above. The metal electric pole outside was standing at a forty-five-degree angle — I could see it from inside the living room, through the hole where the roof had protected this room just ten hours earlier. On the refrigerator were pictures of Sophie's family, hanging there with magnets. In perfect condition. They looked like they hadn't even gotten wet.

I followed Gunner to his room in the back of the house. He stood at the doorway, taking in every square inch of his room. The ceiling was on his bed. The roof was gone. The ceiling fan was hanging from a stud by an electric cord. He seemed so forlorn. Everything was soaking wet.

All he said as he took it in was, "I never had much. Now I got nothing."

Most of the six-foot privacy fence that protected the back yard was gone, some of it was hanging in a tree in the woods behind his place. What was left of his house was naked, for any passerby to see. There were no walls where his garage was. Very few tools were left. And there in the middle of the garage was parked exactly where Gunner left it, was his vintage 1972 Dodge Duster. It was basically unscathed. Except, somehow a toilet found its way to rest against the right rear wheel. But that was it. It was almost funny.

Joe's car and truck were still sitting in front of where the garage had been. They were covered with branches from the large trees that had grown next to the garage. Amazingly, no major branches hit either vehicle. Once the branches were taken off them, they started right up and could be driven away.

The scene, taken in its entirety, was nauseatingly unfathomable. The neighborhood once looked so lush with tall healthy trees, private and inviting. But now it was a place of splinters and broken dreams. Nearly everyone who lived there was displaced, and some would never return.

As the summer went on, I drove through Joe's neighborhood every week or two. Continued total devastation everywhere. It took months to clear off the mangled, impotent trees. They once provided shade and value to homeowners. But they had become nothing more than bits of firewood that no one wanted, because there was so much. I imagined many of the people who called this place home, would survive as they moved forward with their lives. I also imagined many of them would suffer from PTSD and depression well into the future because of the trauma of the storm itself, and it taking months to bring the neighborhood back to life.

● ● ●

Back at my house, things were also in slow motion. We each had different schedules, different food preferences, different basic needs. And loads of dog poop in the back yard.

Joe was sitting on my front porch when I got home from golf the day after the tornado. I sat next to him. He described how Josh was swerving side to side coming up the street as he drove home. He went over the curb when he was parking. Then he stumbled up the driveway, slurring his speech as he answered Joe's questions. Crap. I knew I'd have to deal with his drinking. I wondered what I would do.

The next morning, Wednesday, I picked up Gunner at a friend's house. As I turned on my street, I noticed a beer can just laying there at the end of my street, minding its own business. Josh was the only person I knew who drank that kind of beer. I was starting to get hot. I got home and checked in the red truck that Josh had used. I grabbed the first two empty beer cans I saw in it. I stomped into the house. Josh was still asleep on the air mattress.

I kicked the bottom of his feet till he yelled as he woke up. I threw the cans at him and yelled, "I will not have someone actively drinking alcohol in my house while I have a recovering addict living here. If these are not the last two beers you drink, pack up your stuff and get out of here."

I walked back out of the house and took Gunner to wherever he needed to be.

I don't remember what I actually did over the next few hours. There have been times in my life that I just flat didn't want to go home. This was one of them. I don't particularly enjoy confrontation with family members. Over the years with all the crap I went through with Rick and Ashley, I find it so much easier, more comfortable to not ask a lot of questions. Especially when I'm convinced I won't like the response. It will probably be a lie, anyway. So, when I got a text from Josh asking if he could talk to me, I felt uncomfortable. Dang, he was my Sonny Bunny. I'd talk to him. I didn't know how many more times I'd get to have a conversation with him. Would he accept my resolve with not letting him stay at my house if he continued to drink? Was I being insensitive to his need to drink as he had gone through a life-threatening event: would I be able to kick him out of my house? But wait. Was it really that big of a deal for him to drink? He had been drinking more than half his life, after all. And he was my son. I loved him so much.

As I pulled in my driveway, I didn't know what to expect, and I sure didn't know how I would respond to whatever Josh presented to me. He was sitting on the front porch in the chair Joe occupied the evening before. I parked the car, walked around to the front of the house, and sat in the chair that was unoccupied.

I said, "Josh, I'm willing to talk with you, but you're going to have to walk up the street and pick up the empty beer can over you left by the end of the street before we can have that talk."

Josh defensively stated, a little peeved, "I am not the only person who drinks that kind of beer."

I retorted, "I've lived here for eighteen years, and I've never seen a beer can on my street before. So, you go pick it up and throw it away. Then we'll talk."

Without saying a word, he got up, went in the house to get a plastic bag then took off up the street.

Since he left Joe's house in such a hurry in the aftermath of the tornado, he didn't have socks on. Just his black leather work shoes. I pictured him getting water blisters on his feet like he did at Disney World when he was six or seven years old and didn't wear socks inside his brand-new white high tops.

I wanted to run up to him and tell him, "Never mind. It's OK. Let someone else pick up the can. It's no big deal. We can sit and talk."

I wanted so badly to just spend time with him. He was fading away. And I didn't know what to do.

I held myself back. And watched him trudge up the street, looking pissed off and dejected. My heart hurt. I still didn't know what our conversation would prove to develop into. Twelve minutes later he ambled back toward my house, now looking even more pissed off and dejected. And throw in sheepish. I had a deep knowing he felt backed into a corner with his Momma Llama about to rip him a new one.

He disposed of the beer can in my recycle bin and came up to the porch with not so much confidence as he had when he used to go out for a pass when I threw a football to him in our back yard. I hoped I would have the wherewithal to stick to my guns and insist that he would not be able to stay in my house if he continued to drink. I just could not allow someone drinking in my house while Riley was there, working on staying clean. I took a deep breath as he presented his side.

He talked about how difficult his life was this year. He was really trying to beat his drinking problem. He had no say in his divorce — it just happened — he didn't even sign any paperwork. He felt cheated. He wants his kids back. He wants his wife back. He wants his *life* back.

I listened quietly as he spoke. When he finished, I paused, not knowing what he might expect me to say. Frankly, I didn't know what I expected me to say. Eventually my voice started make sounds. I started talking about how scared I'd been for six years watching, as he atrophied. How concerned I've been when I smelled alcohol — every single time he was near me. How sad I felt as he couldn't keep a job, stay sober, or live with his kids. I told him I didn't want to watch him die; I would not watch him die. His entire body shook as he sobbed.

Then I added, "Josh I can see two possible scenarios for our future. One of them would be Trevor, Liza, and me standing next to your coffin in the near future and Liza asking why you had to love beer more than her."

The sobbing increased.

I continued, "The other scenario is you standing next to my coffin many years from now, and saying, "Thanks Mom. I'm glad I listened to you."

We each had to pause and think about this. And cry some more.

Tears were drying. He whispered, "Can I stay here?"

He would not be able to stay with Joe as Joe had moved in with his girlfriend in a city thirty miles here.

This was hard, but somehow, I got the words out. "No, Josh. I can't let someone stay in my house who is actively drinking while Riley is trying so hard to stay sober. You cannot stay here if you choose to drink."

More sobs. From both of us.

Josh said he understood and would leave. He asked if he could use the red truck. I said no, the truck is not mine. I told him he could use one of my bicycles in the shed. He eventually took off on one of them looking so embarrassed. It felt like he wanted to get as far away from me as possible.

That whole thing was a sucker punch to the gut for me. I loved Josh and cherished every minute I could be with him. To be able to have him under my roof was awesome. And yet my primary goal was to keep Riley safe and sober. Another weird position I found myself in.

The days stretched into weeks. Joe continued to stay with his girlfriend. Gunner stayed with me. I wasn't sure where Josh stayed. He continued to play on Riley's softball team. That team never really did get it together. Man, that was frustrating for everyone involved.

· · ·

One Friday in June I didn't really have a thing to do after I got off work. I decided to go to the cemetery and visit with Rick and his neighbors. I was about to turn onto the road leading to his city of the dead when I got a call from Jasmine, Joe's niece. She sounded very concerned about Josh. Said she didn't know where he was or what he was doing, but something was dreadfully wrong. I was about to tell her I'd go check on him after I visited Rick. She was so persistent in her concern, I decided to turn around and check to see if he was at what was left of Joe's house. I had heard he stayed there sometimes. The addition Joe put on the house was still standing. Well, three walls of it were standing and there was a roof, intact, over the room.

As I continued my journey, I gotta' admit, I was more than a little apprehensive. If Jasmine was right, I wondered what shape Josh would be in when I found him. What if he was dead? Or what if he wasn't there? How would I find him? He wasn't answering his phone. I hate trying to find someone who doesn't want to be found. I gave up on that with Rick. I went down the highway slow, well at least not over the speed limit for a change. I didn't know what I would find. But I knew I wouldn't like it.

I pulled into Joe's driveway. Joe's truck, which Josh had been using was parked along the side of the house, mostly toward the back yard. My God the place looked awful. The places where the roof was gone — like everywhere besides the family room — had huge tarps covering the holes. The tarps were burdened with rainwater from the night before. And hanging low. At some places the tarps had cut loose from where they were tied up, and the loose ends were lazily swaying with the slight breeze.

I parked in the driveway. I got out of the car, even though I didn't want to be there at all. I walked up the sidewalk that Josh had added several years earlier. I didn't want to go inside. There was a sign on the door from some government entity ordering me to stay out — it was condemned. I opened the door with a feeling of trepidation. My legs were quivering in response to the angst I felt. I didn't want to deal with whatever I was about to encounter. I knew I had to go inside and find my son. Dead or alive.

The hard wood floor in the front room was squishy with the four inches of insulation saturated from several more inches of rain since the tornado fractured this house apart. I saw that there was a bit of a walking trail going from the front door, through the front room, then kitchen, and finally to the family room. I tried to stay on the trail, so as not to get my feet soaked from the puddles of water pooled in the drenched insulation. Asbestos. I'm going to die from mesothelioma because I'm there. Funny how I was thinking about that at a time like this.

I rounded the corner into the kitchen. I took in the scene. Josh was lying on the couch, covered with layers of blankets in the ninety-plus degree heat. For a split second, I thought he was unconscious, possibly dead. But his face looked good. Alive, at least. In the next nano second, I could see his eyes were open.

He said, "Hi Mom."

OMG! He was alive. Responsive. Knew who I was. Could talk. Jubilation! Yet, how was he? Really.

I sat next to his head on the other side of the L shaped couch. My breath was stuck. It didn't seem to want to go in or out. My heart was just one big ache. Josh was sweating profusely. I never knew sweat to actually layer, but I swear Josh had four layers of sweat resting on his forehead. More and more sweat bubbling out, through the layers from his skin, like tiny volcanoes swelling upward from a deep place. Bubbling like a slow simmering pan of water. Bubbling from so many places on his head and face. It was a quarter inch thick. He was shivering. I gently placed my hand on his forehead and swiped it across the full length right to left. The sweat was cold. It made no sense. How could he have blankets covering him, in the day's heat, and have cold sweat building up on his face?

I scanned the room for more detail. I hadn't been in Joe's house since the morning after the tornado blew it apart. The family room actually looked in fair shape. The furniture left in it was sort of dry. There was no evidence of any type of alcoholic beverages. Anywhere. Just four or five empty water bottles on the floor in front of Josh.

We chatted about the events of the day. He didn't do a whole lot of anything all day. Drove around. Looking for someplace where he might be able to get work. I asked if he thought he felt like he had a seizure.

He responded, "Yeah, I think I did."

"Do you have your glucometer here?"

"Yeah it's in the truck."

"Ok. I'll go get it." I hated like hell to go to his truck and look for it. I didn't want to find something that I didn't want to find. Like a treasure trove of full and empty beer cans. I opened the passenger side door. He had clothes and toiletries stuffed behind the seat, under the seat, on the seat. No beer cans. I was so relieved. The glucometer was where he said it would be. Another relief. His memory was ok.

I took the glucometer and slowly walked back to the house, taking in the continuing proof of destruction in the back yard that the tornado left behind. I wondered what his blood sugar would prove to be. I wondered what I would do about it. If I had any sense at all I would dial 911 right then and there and get him to the emergency room. But if I did that, they would hydrate him, give him some sugar and keep him overnight. The next day was Trevor's graduation party. No way did I want Trevor to be disappointed because his dad missed the party. And no way did I want Audrey to find out what was going on here. I figured she'd really be pissed. Again. Nope, I would not allow for that to happen.

So, I rationalized that I could do whatever the hospital could do. Even with his blood sugar which was 35. I told Josh I'd go get some orange juice, and protein. As I left, I called Joe and briefed him on the situation. I asked him to go to his house and stay with Josh while I tried to nurse him back to safety. Then I went to the corner store, got orange juice, water, cheese crackers, and peanuts. That oughta' do it. Josh was sitting up a little more when I got back. And Joe was there. They were talking. Nice, easy conversation. Just like they always did in the midst of chaos. Josh started to gobble down the food and juice. He had stopped sweating, so that was good. He ate most of the food, drank all the orange juice, and wanted more. I headed out for more.

When I got back, Josh had checked his blood sugar again. It was edging up to 100. Whew, things were getting better. I breathed a sigh of relief yet continued to feel on edge. We talked a few minutes about our options. We all agreed we'd dodged a bullet. Josh said he felt OK to drive. I wasn't so sure about that. I definitely was not going to get in a vehicle with him driving and head down the highway. We probably shouldn't have done it, but he followed closely behind me through the eight miles home. Once home he settled in on the couch to let his body catch up with what it had been through.

He said he could maybe eat a sub, so I got one with loads of meat. He was sleeping when I got back with it, but eventually he finished the whole thing.

I heard him moving around a bit in the middle of the night and early morning but didn't think much of it and went back to sleep.

When I got up a few hours later, Josh was gone. Crap. Now what? I dialed his number several times. No response.

I came up with some kind of reason to go over to Audrey's place. What a relief to see that Josh was there! Audrey had called Josh early in the morning to report that the kitchen sink was stopped up. Josh went over there and fixed it. There was something wrong with the toilet. He replaced it. The place looked great. Spick and span. Lots of food.

Yet there was a tension in the air so thick you couldn't cut it with a knife. It would take a chain saw. So much had changed in this family that used to have Saturday night dance parties, go swimming at the water park during the summers, and just do everything together. They used to be so happy. Now they barely spoke to each other, unless they were on edge or mad about something. I dropped off what I went there to drop off and left. On the way home I just kept going over and over in my head: What happened to this family?

Once I got home I just kind of wandered around in my back yard, played with Piper a little while. And wondered what happened to *my* family? I did a quick review of my life. Simple, innocent farm life growing up. I so looked forward to raising my kids to be fun, independent, athletic. I really enjoyed watching them grow up, all the sports, all the laughs. I wanted to grow old with my kids coming over to fix things in the house and take care of me. I wanted to play with my grandkids and really get to know them. I wanted to dance at their weddings.

So now with my one son dead and the other one basically absconded from his family, my dreams for my old age were dissipating. Disappearing way too quickly. I still have a great relationship with each of my grandkids and hope to dance at their weddings. Or maybe I'll end up being a wrinkled up, lonely old woman; spending my days in an old folks' home, pooping my pants, crying myself to sleep at night. At that point, that day, there in my back yard, I felt so forlorn I actually saw myself becoming that wrinkled up, lonely, old woman. And I hoped someone would be there to clean me up after I pooped my pants.

Time for the graduation party. I got cleaned up, changed my clothes (No poop in my pants today!) and headed back to Audrey's. The party was more subdued than any I'd ever been to at their house. For one thing, there was no alcohol — that used to be the main course. Also, they were divorced now. Generally, when two people get divorced, there's an obvious rift between the sides of the family. And so it was that day. Josh's side and Audrey's side just pretty much were in different areas. Not much interaction with each other. Well I'm not one to let that get the best of me. I made a point to talk to every single person there. It really was good to see them. I'd had so many good times with each of them over the years.

I can't imagine what Josh was going through. Recent divorce from the only woman he ever loved and continued to love. Decline in respect from his kids because of the times they saw him sloppy drunk. Diabetes. Seizures. Tornado. Whatever that was the day before. I was impressed at how he maneuvered through the entire day. With the house repairs. With interacting with the kids and Audrey's family. And yet I felt so empty for him because of all he'd been through, and what was left of his life.

I wondered what it was like for people who have handicapped children. Always hoping their child will be able to cope with their handicap, get along with other kids, and be able function in society. Of course, he wasn't born with this handicap. Just the tendency for it. He wasn't handicapped until he drank so much his brain insisted he have more. And more. And more. Kind of like what Riley told me — When you're addicted, the thing you need is the thing you know will kill you.

Que sera, sera.

. . .

The rest of the summer is a bit of a blur to me. Joe's homeowner's insurance finally decided to pay his rent in another place. Seems like they first went to a hotel type place, then by maybe August they had a very nice tri-level house in their same town.

I did manage to get out to see a friend in Minnesota toward the end of September. My gawd! It was nice to get away for a few days. I drove by myself, and played golf in South Dakota, Minnesota, and Wisconsin along the way. I'm up to having played in forty-three states now! It really felt good to get away from the tensions of ordinary living, relax with friends I hadn't seen in years, and make a dent in my goal of playing golf in all fifty states.

. . .

In mid-October, I had arranged to do a pedal wagon through parts of town. It was a wagon with places for sixteen people to sit on. The seats on the sides were bicycle seats with bicycle pedals under them. The objective is to pedal through town to different bars and restaurants and stop for refreshments at several of them. Some of my friends, Sophie and some of her friends, and Josh were on it. We had been looking forward to doing this for months.

Josh seemed a little out of sorts. So gangly at six foot five, he reminded me of Ichabod Crane. Gawd, he was skinny. He had a hard time forming words and responding when someone spoke to him. Almost like he'd had a stroke. There was no humor in what he said, when generally he's ridiculously funny. Even his balance was awkward. He fell off his seat several times. I couldn't decipher if his diabetic and neuralgic conditions had suddenly gotten this bad. Or if he was just plain old drunk.

Even with these concerns, we ended up having a really good time.

*　*　*

Of course, as one of my bosses used to say, "Every silver lining has a dark cloud."

Within a few weeks that dark cloud dark cloud would prevail. And more of my family would disappear ….

AND SO, HE GOES

I was at the beauty shop on Wednesday, October 16, 2019 getting the finishing touches on my hair cut. My phone rang. I recognized the call was from the hospital I where I work. It was the emergency room nurse. I've known her for years. She was very direct, stated my son, Josh, fell over backward and fractured his skull from ear to ear. She made a point to tell me it was a basilar skull fracture. She was preparing for him to be care-flighted to the big downtown medical center, Franciscan Hospital. First, she would have to put in an air way. She added it didn't look good. In fact, he could die.

Wow. How could that be? He seemed to have so much fun just three days earlier, on the pedal wagon. Now I had a deep foreboding sense that Josh was really disappearing. Completely. Forever.

I felt heavy and slow as I left the beautician after my hair cut. And yet as I drove to the hospital, I felt like I was floating between the world I know, and the spirit in the sky. Part of me felt lighter than air; part of me felt like I was stuck in quicksand with concrete blocks on my feet. My physical body was lagging behind what I somehow knew was happening to my Sonny Bunny's spirit.

I got to the Franciscan and slogged into the emergency department. My shoes felt like old clodhoppers. Like I used to have to wear as a kid. Hand-me-downs with holes in the soles. And cow shit caked on and dry that I couldn't clean off. It just seemed like I couldn't make my feet move the way I wanted them to. Maybe I was subconsciously slowing down the inevitable.

Josh wasn't at the hospital yet. I meandered listlessly round and round in the waiting room. My body was on high alert. Every muscle tense, as if I might have to jump into some kind action spontaneously. My emotions were past static — more like numb. I saw a Mobil Intensive Care Unit (MICU) ambulance drive by. I went outside and stood near a smaller transfer ambulette. I was frozen in rapt attention as I watched Josh being pulled out of the MICU on a stretcher. The EMTs (Emergency Medical Technicians) were bagging him — forcing air into his lungs through the airway that my friend had placed in his mouth and down his throat. Something was different about the way his skin was laying on his face. It didn't seem to be connected to his muscles. It just seemed to lay there. I had a deep knowing that he was gone already and tried hard as I could to not let that creep into my consciousness. I wondered why he wasn't care flighted as the nurse said he would be. Was his condition so bad that getting him to the big hospital quickly would not make any difference?

The driver of the ambulette was watching along side of me solemnly, slowly shaking her head back and forth, with a sad, worried expression on her face. I looked and her and said, "That's my son they just took off that ambulance."

She said with a deep sadness in her soul, "Oh, that's the one they're taking to … that special room."

I had never heard that expression, but I somehow knew what she meant. I said, "Yeah."

I clumped back inside and continued to revolve about the seating area of the waiting room. With no sense of purpose. What would happen over the next ten days to Josh was an exercise in futility, yet it had to be done.

A middle-aged man dressed in street clothes — dress shirt and a tie — scurried up to me in the waiting room a few minutes later. He verified my identity, then introduced himself as a chaplain. That not only surprised me, it pissed me off. For one thing the first person I talked to in an emergency room should have been a doctor. Or a nurse, at a minimum. Sending a chaplain who had a "Your son is not going to make it." expression on his face was beyond belief. It was just a load of crap as far as I was concerned.

The chaplain said, "Your son is here, and the doctors are working on him. His primary doctor will be out to talk to you in a few minutes. Let me show you to a small private room where he can meet with you."

Joe walked up right then. We went to the room we were led to and sat down, wondering what we would hear. Less than five minutes passed, and the doctor came to talk to us. He told us basically the same thing the chaplain told us and what I heard from my friend at the other hospital. He had a basilar skull fracture which was very serious. They would do more tests to determine the extent of the injury. They would keep us up to date. He left. He seemed to be wrestling with something in his head; distracted by something he knew yet didn't have the human capacity to actually say to us.

The chaplain appeared out of nowhere again and suggested we stay in the room and await further updates. I couldn't stay in that tiny, obscure, claustrophobic room. I needed to be able to move. I needed to be able to look outside. So, I trudged out to the waiting room and meandered around some more. Aimlessly. I had no purpose in life or living right then. All I had to do was wait. Till the next onslaught of bad news came to me.

Here comes the chaplain again. He informed us that Josh was going for a CAT scan and might be rushed up for surgery, so we might not see him for hours. Okay. Sounds serious, yet something they might be able to fix. Maybe I was wrong about him being disappeared.

Well that didn't last long.

Within a few minutes, my daughter Sophie and Josh's ex-wife Audrey were with Joe and me. The head trauma doctor came out and explained some more stuff. Basically, added more detail to what the chaplain said. Josh would go to surgery for a brain bleed.

Again, later, the chaplain approaches, with that "He's not going to make it." expression still on his face. It seemed like he was carefully measuring his words. Words that could not be measured because no matter how they came out, it would be impossible for me to wrap my head around words that could only mean that my son can't live anymore. Even though I still had the deep knowing that he was gone. He said they decided Josh would not go to surgery, instead he would go up to ICU. We would be able to visit him in the emergency room before he would transport to ICU.

My head was reeling. I took that to mean that the injury was so extensive it would be futile to operate. I was so mad I wanted to punch the chaplain in the throat, take him down and shake him. What he said was not what I wanted to hear. And I sure as hell did not want news like that from him. I wanted it from someone who knew what they were talking about. And no, I did *not* want to pray with him.

The four of us were mute as we followed the chaplain to the bed occupied by my son. It was horrible. There he lay. On a vent. The breathing tube that my friend had placed was still down his throat. His arms and legs were twitching kind of like he was having seizures. I'd seen plenty of them and could recognize it. These movements were not seizures. They were uncontrolled, nonsensical, short bursts of slow energy that had no purpose. Pull one knee up. Shake the other one outward. Pull one arm toward his face. Plunge the other down by his side. No rhythm. The stimulation from his brain was disjointed. His eyes never opened. No expression on his face. His son, Trevor, came in. He and his mom hugged. And cried. Joe and I remained silent, stoic, in indescribable pain. Two parents who saw their other son dead in a different emergency room less than three and a half years earlier. Sophie's eyes were filled to the brim with tears. Abruptly, she left the room.

When the time came for Josh to go to ICU, we were instructed as to how to get to his room. Sophie had rejoined us by then. She took me off to the side and said, "How do you and Dad do it? How do you hold it together with Josh in this shape?

The lump in my throat was so big all I could do was whisper slowly, "I don't know."

Joe, slumping as he walked beside me, quietly muttered to no one really, "I probably shouldn't have taken him in and allowed him to keep drinking." He was pretty ripped up about the situation.

Audrey and Trevor went into the ICU room to visit Josh first. When I went in later, I saw multiple IV bottles hanging, monitors were showing his vital signs. Pulse 138, respirations 22, blood pressure 194/102. Not good. Reminded me of when he was about to go through DTs a few years back. I found out his blood alcohol level was zero, and his blood sugar was 127. That was a relief. Josh didn't have any alcohol that dbay and he had his sugar under control. It was clear, punctual proof that he really was trying to get control of his drinking and diabetes. With the results being what they were, what caused him to fall and end up in this shape? Would we ever know?

*   *   *

Autumn is my favorite season. I love to watch the leaves on the trees turn color. I was able to see the beginnings of that in Minnesota the previous month. When I got there, small pockets of orange and yellow peaked through the otherwise all green leaves. I was happy to see out the window in Josh's ICU room. It looked like a thick forest across a parking lot from the hospital. Only one of the trees had a few yellow leaves, some tinged with bright red. My lips curled up in a slight smile when I witnessed the vision. I could still appreciate the beauty of nature in the midst of this upheaval in our basic family identity.

*   *   *

I made sure that the doctors knew his drinking history. When I heard they were giving him Ativan, I informed them it has the opposite effect on him and makes him more agitated. They gave it to him anyway, along with Keppra for seizure control. I don't like that drug either, but they were going to do what they were going to do. So I didn't say else anything about it.

Joe made a sad revelation the next day. He found four small empty vodka bottles in Josh's closet. He added, "I know I was enabling Josh when I took him in and didn't charge him rent. He may have gotten in this condition sooner because I did that. But I just couldn't bear to see him standing on a street corner with a sign, begging for money for food."

I agreed with him and offered comfort. Nothing could ease his anguish right then.

Joe also talked about how when Josh got home from the pedal wagon that Sunday, just three days earlier, he fell and hit his head on the entertainment center. He wanted Joe to look at it because it hurt. Joe never got around to checking it out. Now he felt bad that he didn't look at it. Especially since the doctors found several places in his brain that looked kind of like he'd had some small brain bleeds. Like possible strokes. Hmm, that could explain some things. The tremors. The slow thought processes and speech.

Joe seemed so miserable right then. He and Josh had become best friends over the past few years, and they had so much fun together. They chummed around, threw footballs to each other over the house, had long discussions about sports, and just had fun.

I hurt for him more than I hurt for myself. He would really miss Josh if what I figured turned out to be true. Finally, I said to him, "Josh made his own decisions about whether to drink and smoke. He just couldn't stop. I'm glad you took him in when you did. I would not have wanted to see him homeless either. Yet I couldn't let him drink in my house, especially with a drug addict in recovery living in my house."

Joe nodded his head in agreement, "No, that would have been a bad idea."

⋅ ⋅ ⋅

The next two days I spent much of the afternoons in Josh's room. The doctors made rounds in the morning, so I missed them.

Josh did a lot of twitching; his arms and legs moving, some-times jerking, sometimes moving slow. Sometimes it seemed like the movements had purpose. Mostly they were not meaningful. His right hand was clenched in a tight fist much of the time. He sometimes brought it up toward his face, then back to his waist. His left hand was more open, relaxed and stayed mostly by his side. He chewed on the mouthpiece of the endotracheal tube as if he was trying to spit it out. His eyes were always closed. I opened his eyelids every day and checked to see if his pupils constricted with a light from my phone flashlight shining in them. Every day was different. Sometimes one eye looked outward and the other straight out. Sometimes one eye would constrict a little. It was never consistent with other episodes. It always left me feeling downhearted, empty.

Then the day that Audrey brought Liza to see Josh, his eyes were open much of the time. Man was that weird. His beautiful blue eyes. They were open but they weren't focused on anything. Audrey and I agreed that must have been weird for Liza. We kind of wished they had remained closed while she was there. Still gives me the heeby geebies just to think about it.

Every day following that I got to the hospital around eight o'clock in the morning so I could hear what the different medi-cal specialist teams had to say. Every day I checked his eyes and watched his meaningless movements. Every day brought deeper feelings of sadness and hopelessness. Every day the doctors said it was too soon to tell if he would be able to recover any functioning. Every doc who walked in the room said it just didn't make sense. He should be waking up.

It was unnerving.

. . .

On Saturday things weren't adding up. And all the doctors said so. They continued to report that by all indicators, Josh should be waking up. One doctor repeated that Josh had areas in his brain that looked like past small stroke injuries. Even with that, he should be waking up. It appeared that his brain had experienced an extended period with no oxygen.

I asked one of the docs under what conditions he had witnessed something similar.

He paused a second and replied, "When someone is strangled." Damn.

· · ·

Sunday, Sophie and I were in his room early in the morning. She heard what the doctors said. Then she told me some things that concerned her and her husband. How could a fall from a standing position cause so much damage? What actually happened at that work site? Did anyone witness the fall? Was Josh alone with no attention for an extended time?

We went to the police department to file a complaint.

Small town USA police departments are starkly empty on Sundays. The charge cop did not seem at all interested in doing a thing for us. We persisted. Finally, he took our driver's licenses and disappeared in the back. Next time we saw him, he seemed to have clearly experienced an attitude adjustment. An epiphany of sorts. When he came back to the waiting room, he said he spoke with Josh's nurse who reported that his injury was suspicious. He contacted two detectives who would be in touch with us.

Sophie headed home. I went to the work site where it happened. Josh's car was still there. Joe had gone there to check on it. I didn't look inside because I figured it would be locked. I got a call from one of the detectives. He would be at the police department to interview us in thirty minutes. Sophie and I met him there.

Wow! We sat in the interview room which looked strangely familiar, though I'd never been in there or a place like it before. Sophie pointed out the camera in the corner by the ceiling. Oh yeah. I've seen similar rooms on TV while criminals were being interrogated. I don't remember much of the interview. It's kind of a fog retrospectively. All I know is that I felt I had been heard.

I was relieved. The detective took us seriously. He would go out and investigate the place Josh fell in the morning.

I was in Josh's room when the detective called me on Monday morning. He said he went to the place of the fall and talked to the foreman. He reported that Josh did just fall over from a standing position backward onto a concrete floor. People were there to help him within minutes. The foreman said it seemed like Josh had several minutes of no breathing. He added that he realized it was probably not that long. But it seemed like forever. He reported that Josh continued to have seizures and periods of apnea, until the EMTs got there.

BTW, the detective added, Josh's car was unlocked, and the keys were on the front seat. He locked it and took the keys. Geeze Louise! Only Joe would do that.

. . .

For the previous five days, I had been drawing on my experience working with ICU patients who were on vents. It's customary, according to my memory, that if a patient is intubated five days, that's about the limit. It's time to think of extubating or taking the tube out to see if the patient can breathe on their own. If not, the patient would die. Or the patient would get a trach and be on the vent indefinitely, with the machine breathing for the patient through a hole in their throat. Additionally, a PEG tube would be placed in the stomach for feeding. Then the social workers take charge of getting the patient out of the hospital. And into a long-term care center — for the rest of his breathing life. I talked to Joe about it. I told him of my experience. I didn't want Josh to live as a "vegetable." Joe said he didn't care how Josh remained alive, he just wanted him alive. He would stay with him every day if that's what it took. I pressed him on that. No, he would not want to take care of Josh in his home.

OK. I get it. I could understand Joe's point and didn't argue with him.

When I was alone with Josh on Monday my fears about what might be coming came to fruition. A genuinely nice young doc (looked to be about fourteen) sat on the windowsill next to me and settled in for *the talk*. I don't recall exact words or phrases, but I caught the gist of it. Soon it would be time to make a decision about discontinuing care.

Then another, more seasoned doctor came in and explained things in greater detail. I shook my head with the possibility of each eventuality that he proposed. I didn't want Josh to be breathing on a machine with no chance of him being aware of ... anything. And yet he would continue to ... be. This doctor was trying to tell me that if life support was stopped, Josh would not be the person he was before he fell. He probably would be an invalid possibly a vegetable — for the rest of his days.

So, we would have to decide if we wanted to trach and PEG him and send him to finish his days in a nursing home, unable to respond or interact with anything or anyone. Until some currently unknown infection would overpower the ability of his lungs to expand, his heart to beat. My Sonny Bunny would never know me. Never again relish in the joy of watching Trevor sing in his band. Never toss a softball with me or Liza. Never see Liza graduate from an Ivy League school. Never give Sophie a nagging, hard time, and laugh about it. Never. Never. Never. Too many nevers. No possibilities of an OK life. Just nevers.

I still shake my head thinking of this. Afterall, I felt like I had acknowledged Josh was gone on a deep level when I saw him get off the MICU. My current thinking was that it made no sense to force oxygen into Josh's body in a regular, rhythmic pattern to keep him "alive." There was no proof of life except for his continued vital signs on the screen and his chest going up and down because a machine was forcing air into his lungs in that regular, rhythmic pattern.

· · ·

On Tuesday I drove up to Coldwater and gave two presentations to high school kids. My presentations are called "Addiction. That won't happen in my Family. Right?" They start out with general information about drugs and addiction. I read excerpts from my other book, *"Destination ... Sanity."* At the end of these two presentations, I added a short story about Josh. I talked about him being an alcoholic, losing his job, losing his house, losing his wife, and continuing to drink through it all. I talked about him falling and being in a coma for nearly a week. I talked about there soon being two empty chairs at our dinner table. There was not a dry eye in either audience of three hundred-plus kids each. I was flabbergasted. Was I actually having an impact on these kids? Would they remember what I said and make smart decisions when it came to their own drug and alcohol use?

Then I went back to the hospital to visit Josh for several hours.

* * *

The next day, a week after he fell, the doctors called for a meeting to discuss discontinuing life support. Hospital staff calls such a meeting a "family meeting" — they meet with the family. I understood that. I've set up many of them myself at the hospitals I work at. So, I told Joe and Sophie we would have a family meeting and the time. Well that was confusing for them. Why would our family have to go to the hospital to talk to each other? I explained to Joe that the ICU staff would be there along with the palliative care person. Funny how people who know, aren't always clear with people whom they think also know, but don't know.

We met on Thursday. Joe, Sophie, Audrey, Trevor, Liza, and I. It was very emotional for each of us. Yet we all agreed to begin comfort measures only. Since Josh and Audrey were divorced, she felt that she should not be the one to sign the papers. I had encouraged her to go to the meeting as Josh probably talked to her more than any of us concerning his end of life wishes. I'm glad she reconsidered and joined us. Sophie was the first alternate listed on Josh's Durable Power of Attorney document. She would be the one to sign the papers. I was second alternate. Geez the expression on Sophie's face when she realized what this all meant! She was stunned, yet, took on the responsibility with a sense of pride and love for her brother.

Trevor and Liza were so mature. Liza was attentive and at times a good distraction for the rest of us — she tried to make a house out of the business cards on the table. Intermittently, she would sit up straight and make a point. At fourteen, she was incredibly mature.

Trevor was asked several important questions that, by rights as the adult son, he was in the place to make certain decisions. He agreed to stop treatment, he wanted to donate his dad's organs so his dad could live on in others, and he wanted his body cremated. That is a tough spot for a kid who graduated from high school just six months before that. He grew up a lot in a short time. He voiced understanding of the situation and what was at stake. He had talked to Josh about his wishes and demonstrated that he would want those wishes carried out. In that moment, he took charge of the conversation and decision making.

Life support would be discontinued twenty-four hours after Sophie signed the paper. Hospice would then be in charge of his care.

After the meeting, Audrey, Trevor, and Liza spent some time with Josh, then we other three went into the death room. Beginning then, there would be no limit on the number of visitors. The hospitality cart was brought out. I cringed when I saw it. It's a cart that has drinks and snacks on it for the family when death of a patient in that room is eminent. I thought I knew sadness. That day I understood it even more. On a level so deep it roiled me to my core. My remaining son would soon officially be dead, too.

· · ·

The next day, Friday, Sophie and I met with the organization that would be responsible for harvesting Josh's organs. (I still hate that phrase.) The two people seemed knowledgeable about their roles, though new at their jobs. After a very lengthy conversation about Josh's recent travel and possible sexual encounters (For starters: Did he have relations with anyone or anything in Africa? Sophie was embarrassed to say the least. She said, no. Josh did not recently have sex with a monkey.) The agreement was that, following his death, Josh would be picked up by the coroner's office for an autopsy. Then the organ donation team would pick him up for the organ extraction. I asked specifically if his organs could all be used since he was diabetic, and alcoholic. They studied his labs a bit and said that could all be used. That surprised me. I really didn't think they could take his liver or pancreas. I couldn't imagine an alcoholic, diabetic would have usable organs for someone. But they assured me all organs would be harvested and used if they could locate a donor.

Seemed like a well-oiled plan. I had every confidence that Josh would live on in multiple people because they got his organs. Till the end of their time. Course they might wonder why they had such a dry sense of humor all of a sudden. Most importantly, I felt that his kids' wishes would be realized.

Sophie and I went back to his room. Not sure what we were going to do once we got there. Ever since the beginning of this nightmare, Sophie had been punching Josh when she visited and telling him she'd had enough of this act, and he should wake up. Now, we all agreed, there was no hope in Josh recovering. No point in punching him anymore. He could take it. He couldn't give it back.

A few minutes later, my grandson, Hunter and his girlfriend came in. Then Jasmine, Joe's niece, who was already quite emotional. She knew she had to say good-by to her cousin who had become a best friend, and confidant.

Shortly, two respiratory therapists (RTs) came in. They glanced at us in the room, then ignored us. They spoke very little after that and went to work on him. They turned off the vent machine. They took the tape off Josh's endotracheal tube where it was taped to his face and started to pull on it. For a split second, I wanted to stop them. I wanted to smack them around because I knew that what they were about to do would result in the death of my son. Then smoothly, in less than the time it takes to take a breath, the tube was out. They pulled it out as if it was just another thing. Sophie and I quietly watched with saucers for eyes. And water spickets pouring tears down our cheeks.

Hunter and his girlfriend were quiet. Eyes in disbelief at how much tubing had been down Josh's throat.

Jasmine was pacing and crying. Expressing mumbled, emotional, guttural pain that came out in fits and starts. She was expressing what the rest of us held in.

Josh was almost unrecognizable without the blue tube that had kept him alive for ten days. Suddenly the tube felt like his lifeline not the dreaded monster it had felt like. And it was out. He coughed for several minutes, never opening his eyes. I half expected him to sit up and start yelling at the RTs. But no, he just lay there, eventually quieted down. And breathed on his own. For now.

We all silently left after a few more minutes and continued with our day.

I visited for a short time on Saturday. I thought about how Joe and I had watched the Buckeyes game right there in that room just a week before. Josh seemed even more relaxed this day, if that's possible. No movement. No response. His eyes were clouding over. And he was breathing on his own. His vital signs were slowing down. All of them.

It was Sophie's birthday. I hoped he wouldn't die today.

. . .

I had been watching the leaves on the trees outside Josh's window change from mostly dark green to mostly orange, yellow and red over the course of his stay in the hospital. The night before, a terrible storm came through and took most of the leaves with it. Today it was dreary outside. The trees appeared somehow dismal

There were lots of naked branches that seemed to be shivering in the cold.

. . .

Josh made it to Sunday. I stopped by mid-morning. Any sadness I'd felt through the past four and a half years related to Josh getting sicker and sicker was multiplied astronomically when I walked into his death room. I could hear him breathing out in the hall. He sounded like Darth Vader. Such a dry heavy breath. Almost like a loud snore. His cheeks were shallow. His mouth so dry, parched. Did anybody even do mouth care on him? Did they just leave him alone because he was about to die anyway? His vital signs were almost non-existent. 78/62, 48, 12. I knew he would last only a few hours at best.

I couldn't bear to see him like this. I told him just a few months ago, that I would not watch him die. But what had I been doing for ten days if not watching him die? I managed to stay only a few minutes. For the first time during this entire conundrum I could not speak to any of the staff. I could not sit with my Sonny Bunny. Not even for one minute. I bent over his bed and hugged him as best I could. I kissed his forehead. I said good-by. I left that ICU. For the last time.

Sophie had stopped by after I left. Then she came over to my house. Riley came over as well. At about 1:40, Sophie got a call from the hospice nurse. It would happen soon. Within a half hour. Did she or anyone else want to be there when Josh passed? I said no. Seemed like a stupid question. Who wants to watch their son die? Sophie didn't want to be there either.

. . .

He took his last breath on this earth a few minutes later. He may have been alone in his room. I could not watch him die. I could not.

. . .

Even though I felt he was gone eleven days earlier, I was dumbfounded when I heard the indubitable reality. Sophie got the call. I knew what they were saying by the expression on her face.

You can't fake finding out your brother just died. You can't fake death. We were silent. Then we floated toward each other and melted together and cried for a brief few minutes.

It was over. I felt defeated. I felt empty. I felt like part of my soul had been ripped out of me. My son was dead. What the hell. Deep tremors wrecked my bones, my soul. Josh was sucked out of my living. He was totally gone. The disappearing was over. He was disappeared.

. . .

The abject sense of aloneness I felt was indescribable. I remembered feeling him move in my womb. He'd put his feet up under my ribs and push them outward till they were in a permanent fixed outward position, where they remain today. I remembered all those days of practicing sports in our back yard. I remembered how easy school was for him — he was so damn smart. I remembered his temper. And most of all I remembered his joy. He was such a happy kid, filled with orneriness. He loved his wife. He was such a proud, happy dad.

. . .

I imagined getting myself out of a big empty, vault right then. I closed and locked the door behind me. It's a solemn place where only I can go to be with Josh. A hallowed place where I can be me with him and he can be him with me. Where every memory is current with the time it happened. It's a divine place reserved for a mother and the child she birthed. No one else can interrupt or intrude upon the sacredness of that space. But now he's gone. I can still go there. But it just won't be the same. Old memories, with no hope of making new ones. What's the point?

. . .

Joe sent a group text including Josh, a little after two o'clock to let us know that the Bengals had scored! Oops, I guess we better start telling people Josh is gone.

About seven that evening, everyone was gone from my house. My sister Ginger texted me — how are things going? Dang I told

Joe but I never told anybody else that Josh was dead. Guess I forgot. I called her. She had gone up to see him and wasn't permitted in. I told her the story. Unemotionally. Matter-of-factly. I couldn't know why I wasn't crying. I just didn't feel like it. I still don't.

* * *

I felt at peace, home alone. Nothing to do but relax. The struggle was over. Josh was gone. As the afternoon went on into the evening, my head was following Josh where I imagined his body would be. Probably have his corneas removed quickly, and they would go in someone else's eyes by tomorrow. Someone will be able to see! Awesome! Following that, by my understanding, he would go for an autopsy. Then to Life Connections where additional organs would be harvested. Or maybe it was the other way around. I couldn't remember.

Sophie called me at about 8:45 and said Life Connections had called to request having the funeral home pick up the body. What?! For some reason, I thought he would stay there till morning. I thought that's about how long it would take. I called Life Connections and ripped that poor girl who answered the phone a new one.

"Did he have the autopsy?"

"No."

"How long did he stay in ICU?"

"I don't know."

"When was he picked up from the hospital?"

"8:30."

"Were his organs harvested?"

"No."

I was seething. They promised Sophie and me that his organs would live on in others. And I promised Josh's kids. Well it was too late now to keep that promise.

I collected my thoughts, and put my emotions in check then I called the charge nurse at the ICU. She said she didn't know where Josh's body was. He was gone when she started her shift at seven pm.

I called the coroner's office and reaffirmed that, no, Josh did not go there for an autopsy.

OK so now I was really pissed off. I promised Josh's kids he would live on in others. Now I'm led to believe that none of his organs were taken. I felt sick. Disappointed. Confused. And pissed. The only thing that made sense to me was that Josh died at an inconvenient time. Sunday afternoon. I figured Life Connections didn't have enough staff on Sundays to take care of business the way they promised Sophie and me. Why else would his body just lay there till it was too late to use any of it?

I called my boss to vent. She knows I seldom complain, so she took me seriously. And gave me the name of the patient rep at the Franciscan. I immediately emailed Andi all of the above information. I said it was bad enough to have lost my son to death, but to have his body lost after his death was more that I could accept.

I finally went to bed, feeling I had let Josh down. He always trusted me. I always kept him safe. I pictured him as a kid, wanting to cuddle with me, and looking up at me with so much love.

Then his expression changed to more like a confusing question, "Can't you make this right Momma Llama?"

With that, the picture I had of him in my mind disappeared as in a puff of smoke. I had to make it right.

On Monday, I got a call from Andi's employee. He announced who he was and asked what Josh's birthdate was. I told him, and he hung up. No offers of condolences. No, we'll get back with you. Just goodbye. Ok, that was odd.

On Tuesday I got a call from someone else from Andi's office. This woman was curt and to the point. No condolences. No, "How are you?" Just a dry interpretation of what happened. Josh died. He went to the morgue. Life Connections picked him up. I asked several questions. She got defensive. I knew I wasn't getting anywhere, so I hung up.

By Wednesday I'd talked with the coroner's office in the county where he fell and notified them that Josh died. They would have no further reason to be involved. I also had three conversations with the coroner's office in the county where he died. I came to understand that they did not do an autopsy because the tests that were done in the hospital were more definitive than any information they could glean by taking actual tissue samples. OK. I can understand that. But it sure as hell didn't answer my questions about why Life Connections wasn't able to do anything with his organs. I still felt like Josh's body had been lost for six or seven hours.

I emailed Andi with my observations. I added that the two employees who called would perhaps benefit from some interpersonal communication training for better customer satisfaction. She emailed back and asked if we could talk. I said no. I was not in a state of mind to discuss this. She could continue to email me as she would like.

Her email was very detailed. She'd spent the entire morning with ICU staff. They remembered Josh. After he died, a floor nurse accompanied his body to the morgue. Things were done very respectfully, as is the case with every person's body following their death. She had no explanation why he didn't have an autopsy. She couldn't tell me when he left the morgue. I was done with her.

After more emails, and more confusing information, all I found out was that his skin and bones were harvested. I still don't know why his organs were left. If I ever get an answer, I'll let you know.

THE FUNERAL

While all this was going on, Joe and I made funeral arrangements at Routsong Funeral Home. I didn't tell Joe about the issues following Josh's death. It was agonizing. I had written up the obit which was accepted with just a little proofing. We would have a viewing on Friday evening, with the funeral Saturday morning. The side room would be open. The Moose would have a ceremony after the viewing. There would be a minister to open the service Saturday. I would do the eulogy. Sophie and Trevor would speak.

* * *

I was the first one to arrive to the funeral home for the viewing. The funeral director, TR, met me at the door. He and his staff were still doing last minute prep. I slowly, sadly walked through the entry, and rounded the corner to see my son in a casket. Dammit. At a glance, I could tell, he was beautiful.

And he was dead.

My gaze continued. My legs got weak. They didn't work. I could not move any closer. I felt hobbled in place. Just like that, TR was at my side, took my hand and walked a few steps with me. Closer to my dead son. Then he let go of my hand and silently urged me forward. By then I was mesmerized by my son lying in a casket. No amount of condolences and support can take away the paralyzing shock of a mother seeing her son in a casket.

I had already appreciated that TR had placed an autumn floral arrangement with OSU and Bengal ball caps on top of the foot of his casket, a softball and glove by his side, and the orange bowl that Liza made in grade school at his head. It had survived a tornado and at least six moves in the last three years.

By the time I got to the casket all I could do was marvel at how beautiful Josh was as he lay there. Normally he had a goatee — ever since high school. Now he had the additional beard growth that accumulated while he was in the hospital. It struck me as weird somehow, that his beard continued to grow while he was in the hospital. He couldn't even breathe on his own.

I stood there. I touched his hands, his chest. I held his face in my hands. I kissed his forehead. I was lost in time, leaning over my dead son ... cloaking him with my love and grief.

. . .

Although Trevor and Liza were not all that up on having two days of funeral stuff, they did great and I think they appreciated how things turned out. We stood by Josh's casket Trevor at the head, then Liza, me, Joe, and Sophie. I wondered how upset they were by Josh's passing at such a young age. How terrible for them. Yet I knew they understood their dad's disease processes. They had watched his decline for years. They seemed to accept his death. My God. How awful.

People started coming in right at five o'clock. Lots of my family made it, some of them drove over eighty miles to be sad with me and offer their strength. (I'm pretty sure they all complained about the traffic.) Almost everyone in my department at work were there. Even the president of the hospital. (He might have felt like he needed to, because I beat him in golf a few years ago!!) Loads and loads of my friends came — people I've known since first grade, and people I've met in golf leagues in recent years. Many people from the Moose that Joe goes to were there. I was impressed that Trevor and Liza's teachers came. There may have been close to two hundred people there. I think I knew all but maybe ten of them.

I'm so glad we had the funeral events at Routsong. TR does an awesome job at funerals. I absolutely love that he opened the side room at the funeral home for folks to sit, visit and share stories. They could have a light meal, and some beverages. I overheard a lot of people say they never experienced that before. Generally, it's walk in, wait in line, shake hands, offer condolences, leave.

Jasmine made a video of pictures of Josh as a kid and growing up. She also added quotes of people talking about him. People stopped in their tracks entering the funeral home just to stand there and watch the video. It was an awesome video.

We made it to seven o'clock. People were still coming in. TR encouraged everyone to sit down. The Moose fellows walked up in suits that they might have outgrown in the beginning of this millennium. It was interesting. Each of them had their prepared words to say, then each of them placed a white rose on Josh's chest. I'm sure this ceremony was very meaningful to Joe. He has been very involved with the Moose fraternity — all the Christmas parties and Easter egg hunts for kids, all the administrative things he did, all the times he and Josh met there in recent years, all the lifelong friends he made there — never considering that those people would offer him solace at his son's funeral.

I went into the community room and shared some wine with TR and some of his staff. It's comforting to be around friends in a place like that, when it's your son's death folks are there for. When I went into the main room, I realized everyone was gone. That was weird. I wonder if they thought I left without saying good-by. So, I went home and got ready for the next phase.

In the morning, I was the first one there again. This time I walked up to the casket without pausing. The wretched, yet all too familiar, sadness was overwhelming. I stood there by his side, tears welling up in my eyes, but not spilling out. My God, how could this be? Both my sons gone. I gazed at Josh. Touched his face. Oh, how I yearned to hold his living body.

People started coming in. I took my spot in the receiving line. Trevor, Liza, Joe, Sophie soon by my sides. So many people coming in. Then TR directed them to take a seat. I believe there were over a hundred and fifty seats. They were all taken. Standing room only in the back. Wow.

The preacher started out. He welcomed everybody, adding how wonderful it is to have so many people there. He called it a "holy collision." I liked that. I didn't really care for the way he talked about me for such a long time. What a strong woman I am. I don't even know what that means. So. Whatever.

He introduced me. This is what I said:

It seems like I just did this.

Often in the past, as a nurse and social worker when I've been in sad situations with families, I've said, "It's OK to cry. In fact, the more you cry the less you'll have to pee." So, let it rip if you want to. You'll be right there with me. Crying from the heart.

"This is the day the lord has made. Let us rejoice and be glad in it."

Today is the day we celebrate the life of my son, Josh. My religious upbringing in the Catholic faith was all about rejoicing the times of our lives. Joe's belief system is centered on — God is love. And to be close to God, we must love each other. We had a lot of rejoicing and love in our house as the kids were growing up.

I can't think of anyone filled with more love and rejoicing than Josh. Sure, he was a little shit as a kid. He was full of energy and orneriness. Always stretching the boundaries. Always wanting more excitement. Like one day I let the three kids go to the park by themselves for the first time. It was a cold day. But the sun was shining. What could go wrong? I thought they would stay on the playground equipment or ride their bikes in the parking lot so I could keep an eye on them from my front picture window. I looked away for like, one minute, and here comes Josh walking up the road, soaking wet. He saw ice on the creek and wanted to see what it looked like from the bottom. He got a quick look, before he fell in.

He loved to climb trees. One evening, we were sitting on the back patio, and we heard Josh shouting down to us. At first, we couldn't figure out where he was. Finally, we saw him at the top of the maple tree out front. 70 feet high. Waving his hand above the topmost branch. Freaked me out. I let him have it. He could climb as high as the house, but not any further. He didn't get it. Finally, I said, "If you're as high as the house and you fall, you'll probably just break a bone. If you fall from the top of the tree, you could die." He still went up to the top every chance he got.

He had lots of owies. And he learned to not complain about stuff like that because complaining generally made things worse. Except once he cut his knee open. He wrapped it up as best as he could and didn't say a word to me — so he could play football that night. Gees when I finally saw the extent of the injury after the game, I realized he should have had, probably, 20 stitches! Oh well. They beat Fairborn. So ...

One of Josh's claims to fame happened when he fell at the elementary school he went to. He was chasing a football, tripped, and broke his collar bone. Because of that, playing football is still not allowed at that school. He also climbed a rope that was attached to the rafters in the gym. He didn't stop with that. He grabbed the rafter and took off along the ceiling. The gym teacher was really freaking out till Josh decided to come down — using the rope. I don't think I never saw a climbing rope hanging in the gym after that. He sounded so innocent as he gave me his version — it was easy, so why not go for it?

Sports. Mmm. He loved sports. He was going to be the next Bo Jackson. Only he planned to add basketball to his repertoire of football and baseball. I played catch with him seems like every night. I loved every minute of it. He played pee wee football 5th and 6th grade. After the last game he came out to the car and kicked the back tire. I said What's wrong? He said, "You should have let me play in 4th grade!" He always wanted more. Reality set in and he realized he probably wouldn't go pro. So he settled into softball. With gusto. He loved softball. And we loved watching him play.

He grew fast. And a lot. I'll never forget standing at the kitchen sink and he was next to me, probably 8th grade.

I tried to correct him about some dumb thing he did. Pointed down then pointed up. Whew he tall!

His first was car was a Dodge Aries. He and his brother Rick dug it out of a big pile of snow in his grandma and grandpas' back yard. It was a beauty. Josh said if they floored it going downhill with a stiff tail wind, they might be able to get it up to 60 in a little more than a mile. Josh's first date with Audrey was in the Aries. As it turns out the car wasn't in all that good a shape. She had to get up under the hood to change gears from reverse to drive. That was the result of the boys' creative mechanics. They rigged up the gear shifter thing with a vice grip and duct tape. That was the only way they could switch gears. Those two were something when they put their heads together!!

One day Josh found a wrecked Cadillac in an impound lot. Somehow, he and some friends finagled a check from Joe, and they got the car out. They towed it to our house, couldn't get it started, so they towed it to his friend Matt's house. His mom got a little upset when they lit a fire in their garage under the car to try to thaw out the frozen block. She had the car towed off their property. And back to our house. Eventually when the brakes didn't work, the car rolled down the driveway and into the neighbor's yard. The neighbors complained about it and the car was towed back to the impound lot. End of Josh's first Cadillac. End of story.

This time of year was always special for Josh. His birthday, October 30, was the same day as trick-or-treat night. He thought it was so cool that he would get to pick a place to go out to eat, then walk around the neighborhood and people gave him candy. Score! One year, we had the stupidest dog known to mankind. Ozark was his name. When we got home from Josh's birthday's dinner, Ozark had somehow gotten Josh's cake from the top of the refrigerator and ate the whole thing. Then through the night he found Josh's candy stashed behind the couch and ate every piece. Every candy bar. Even got the suckers off the sticks without completely taking off the wrapper. Probably three pounds of chocolate, and it still didn't kill him!

Josh still liked dogs after that. Denali was his favorite as a kid. And the last 14 years it's been Lassie — he got her the same year Liza was born.

Another Halloween, Josh and Rick tried to really scare the little neighborhood kids while I was spending the evening with my mom. They had dummies out in the yard. And dressed as dummies themselves. Rick was slumped on the front porch. Josh was hiding up in that same tree he liked to climb in the front yard. As the little kids came close, Rick would jump up screaming, and Josh fell out of the tree. He had been attached by rope to the tree by a block and tackle, so the plan was for Rick to keep a tight hold on the rope so Josh wouldn't smash into the sidewalk. It worked, for the most part. Really scared the little kids. In fact, now that I think of it, we had very few trick-or-treaters for years after that.

One of the very best things I ever did with Josh was to take a vacation with just him. We went to a dude ranch in Montana. He had never been on a horse before and was a little perplexed as to why I would MAKE him do that. We had sooo much fun. The memory of seeing him run his horse full speed through the sage, chasing cows still makes me laugh. It was a major conversation topic for years.

Josh cared very much for his little sister, Sophie. He had a strange way of showing it early on. In fact, Sophie tried to keep her distance from Josh as much as possible when they were little. She'd like to talk a little about that herself.

Sophie started out by saying that Josh made her the person she is. He taught her how give a punch — and how to take one. He taught her how to play the tackle game. One of them would stand in the middle of the room and the other would tackle that person. As it turns out she was the one who always stood in the middle of the room. And got tackled. Go figure.

He taught her the rules of football. He taught her how to punch, spit, and cuss.

Sophie's soliloquy was awesome. She had pauses at just the right places. She made people laugh, even as she grieved.

> About 12 years ago Josh explained something amazing to me. He said: When I got married, I was surprised at how much I loved Audrey. I did not know I could ever love anyone like that. I didn't think I had enough love in me for another person. Then we had Trevor. I love Trevor more than myself. Finally, Liza came into our lives. I have so much love for her, it blows my mind." He rejoiced in his family and loved them so much.
>
> Trevor has some memories.

What a treat to hear Trevor talk about his dad and what he learned from him. What a great young man Trevor has grown to be.

> Joe and Josh shared some amazing experiences this past year. On Memorial Day, their house got blown away in the tornado that destroyed their neighborhood. As Gunner was facetiming with his friends the ceiling and roof blew off his bedroom above him. Josh and Joe were getting jostled around in the living room. Josh eventually landed in the hallway with the ceiling and roof on top of him. Joe was in the living room under similar debris. The three of them had an incredible summer. Living in different places as they tore down the old house and got ready for the new one. And wouldn't you know — the house went up yesterday. And will be ready for move in before Christmas.
>
> Something that has guided me through many hardships in my life is a book by Kahlil Gibran called *The Prophet*.
>
> I want to read the chapter titled On Children:
>
> *Your children … are the sons and daughters of life's longing for itself.*
> *They come through you but not from you.*

And though they are with you they do not belong to you.
You may give them your love but not your thoughts.
For they have their own thoughts.
You may house their bodies but not their souls.
for their souls dwell in the house of tomorrow
which you cannot visit not even in your dreams.
You may strive to be like them but seek not to make them
*   like you*
for life goes not backward nor tarries in yesterday.
You are the bow from which your children
as living arrows are sent forth.
The archer sees the mark upon the path of the infinite
and He bends you with His might that his arrows may go
*   swift and far.*
Let your bending in the archer's hand be for gladness;
for even as he loves the arrow that flies
so He loves the bow that is stable.

People say things to Joe and me about how awful it is to
lose both of our sons. They're right. It is awful to lose 2 sons
before their 40th birthdays. Well I'm so glad we had them as
long as we did. They filled our lives with so much love and
rejoicing. And they added 6 children to our world. Along
with our other 2 grandkids and Joe and I have a lot to be
grateful for.

Our lives are changed forever. Trevor and Liza, please
remember the fun-loving guy your dad was. He had his challenges. And he struggled to manage them. None of this makes
sense now. You weren't supposed to lose your dad so soon.
I'm sure he didn't want to go. Yet he's gone. And you are left
to wonder why. You two have been given many gifts — gifts of
music, superior intellect, strong bodies, strong will power, and
amazing senses of humor. You can accomplish great things in
your lives. You got this!

One of my favorite Bible verses includes this:

There is a time for everything, and a season for every activity under the heavens.

A time to be born and a time to die

A time to weep and a time to laugh.

A time to mourn and a time to dance.

We are in a time to mourn Josh's death. We are also here to celebrate his life. His life of rejoicing and love.

May Josh's soul, and the soul of his brother Rick, their cousins Mark and all the souls of the faithful departed rest in peace. Amen.

On que, TR started to play "The Rose" by Bette Midler. I had a vase with yellow long stem roses in a vase up front. I gave one to Trevor, then Liza, Joe, Sophie, Riley, Gunner, Hunter. With each one given, we hugged. Joe and I hugged and cried for a good bit. Then I placed a rose on Josh's hands, held his face, kissed his forehead. This time the tears dropped on him.

Sophie and Trevor added so much to our celebration of Josh's life.

As I spoke, I witnessed faces of love staring back at me. More tears from them. More sorrow. And fortunately, laughter. Laughter was especially loud when Sophie spoke. Man she was funny.

Then folks started coming up to me with more hugs, and words of comfort. I tried to sift through them to get to the people at the back who had been standing this whole time. I was impressed that Sophie's in-laws came from as far away as Cleveland. Audrey's family were all there as well. I appreciated that. Even though Josh and Audrey were divorced, her family still cared for Josh. They were all there. I felt so close to them.

. . .

Most people there joined in for the continuing celebration at the Moose Lodge. The food there was amazingly delicious. They opened up a separate bar in the dining section, and Joe paid for beverages for all. Joe's best friend, Phil, suggested passing the bucket to collect donations for Trevor and Liza's college funds. That ended up being a huge success. I think I talked to every person there. Finally, the only people remaining were some of my dearest friends. We sat and enjoyed living over many drinks.

. . .

Then the day was done. I went home. And relaxed. And relived the day minute by minute.

MOVING FORWARD

So what can I say after that story?

. . .

Well, the story continues. During the seven workdays following Josh's funeral, Riley went to work and made it through just a half day. She wouldn't talk to me. Just stayed in bed, occasionally coming upstairs to get a bite to eat, some fluids, use the toilet. I'm all about allowing someone to grieve the way they need to grieve. This was beginning to feel like something other than grieving. Finally, on the tenth day after the funeral, I'd had enough. I felt like I had to do something to get her up and active. I feared she was sinking into a deep depression and would soon be drifting into a permanent sleep.

Riley had been getting up about 6:30 to leave for work by seven. I wanted to make sure she got to work, but since she slept in the basement and I sleep on the first floor, I didn't really care to wake her up in person. So, I called her at 6:30 to tell her it was time to get up. She sounded great. Her voice was clear and strong.

She said, "Ok grandma, I'll get up."

I thought, "Ok, that's great."

Then I waited. About seven I called her again. Again, she sounded clear and strong. "I don't have to be there till eight today, grandma."

I waited some more. No movement from the basement. I'd had enough. I went downstairs and turned on all the fluorescent lights down there. I sat on her bed and asked if she was OK. She wasn't particularly happy with me and started to let me know how she felt. she was loud about it, even though I was standing right there next to her.

I said, "Oh no you don't. Don't you be yelling at me."

She was up out of bed and moving. I said, "Riley, I don't know what's going on here …. No wait, I think I do know what's going on. You need to figure out how to get to work, on time, every day."

"I know, grandma!"

I went back upstairs and made my coffee. A little while later, I noticed all the lights were off downstairs. It was quiet. I yelled down to her that I was going out to run some errands. Frankly, I just wanted to get out of my own house and think about what to do about this development. No response from the bottom of my house. I left, feeling confused.

• • •

When I got home a few hours later, I noticed I had a text from Riley. It read:

> Grandma I died the weekend Josh was in the hospital and I had to be narcaned several times. I was in the same hospital he was in. I called a friend who is a nurse. She's going to take me to get in residential treatment.

A breeze could have knocked me over right then. She died? She had to be narcaned several times? Was she really going to admit herself into treatment? I believed what she said about overdosing, dying, and being in the hospital. What I had a hard time believing was that she was getting into a treatment center. I had been checking availability at every treatment facility I could think of for the past week. I'd been calling everybody I could think of who might have a suggestion. No place had an open bed. I had a hard time imagining that she could walk into a place and have a bed waiting for her, with treatment to start immediately.

I slumped into a chair and thought about what to do. For days I thought about what to do. I didn't know where she was. I didn't know if she was telling the truth about getting into a treatment center. I didn't know if Riley was lying to me and was going to move in with someone who would help her stay stoned

I did know fear. Would Joe and I be planning yet another funeral before Thanksgiving?

Then finally, I heard from Riley. She was in a safe house. She wasn't getting treatment there, but she could stay at this place till a treatment bed opened up for her, as long as she didn't use any drugs. She sounded good. I was allowed to drop off some stuff for her — clothes, hygiene supplies. I wasn't allowed to see her, or talk to her.

* * *

We celebrated Thanksgiving at my place, missing Josh and Riley. I could almost see him and hear him making wise cracks about silly stuff going on in my back yard. Playing sports in the back yard just wasn't the same without them, especially not seeing Riley popping the volleyball around. Jasmine came over too. I'm so glad she was there. She kept the older grandkids entertained in the kitchen. Apparently, they were talking about how the Welkamp name is jinxed. Nobody could make it to forty. I wish I could have gotten in on that! It was good that we got together. We needed it. We laughed and played.

* * *

There were still some things to take care of with the funeral home. Liza wanted a locket with Josh's ashes inside. I ordered two scattering tubes for Trevor and Liza. They hope to go to the Caribbean together to scatter the ashes at some point.

Everything was ready to pick up the day we were getting together for our Christmas party. I talked to TR's son for a minute, then carried the urn and scattering tubes out of the funeral home. I didn't even get to my car before I teared up and finally sobbed. I was carrying my Sonny Bunny home. I never liked the idea of cremation. I don't know, it just didn't feel right to burn somebody up. My heart hurt when I knew the exact time it was happening to Josh. But that day, holding the urn in my arms, I was so glad we decided to cremate his body. I felt so close to Josh. I walked in the house and sat in Pop's old rocking chair. He and Mom got it for a wedding gift back in 1929. Josh always claimed it should rightly go to him because he used to crawl under it and play with the springs. I rocked and I cried, and I rocked, and I cried. I felt so close to Josh, and I also kind of felt wrapped up in Pop's arms.

The moment was short lived. People would be coming over soon. I needed to cook. So I made a little altar in front of my picture window in the living room. I put the purple velvet bag that held the urn on a small table, then the urn with a scattering tube on either side.

Trevor and Liza came first. I was glad. I walked them into the living room and showed them the urn their dad was in. They seemed to appreciate it. I got some great hugs.

Sophie came next. Her kids and Josh's kids were playing with her husband in the back yard. I took Sophie into the living rom. She glanced at the altar, stopped in her tracks, and asked, "Is that Josh?"

"Yes."

We hugged and cried. Then I directed her to sit in that same rocking chair I had been in. I gently placed the urn on her lap. She caressed it. Tears began to flow down her cheeks. I was emotional as well. I left her alone. And went outside to give her some time to be alone with her big brother.

A few minutes later, she came outside looking for me. I was in the back yard with a shovel. Sophie still had tears keeping her face moist. She walked determinedly toward me, smiling through the tears.

"So you left me there holding Josh to come out here and shovel dog shit?"

I laughed. We hugged and cried some more. In the backyard. With Piper running circles around us.

"Josh weighs the same in that urn as a baby that size would weigh."

I agreed.

We hugged there in the middle of my back yard. Everything else disappeared. I couldn't hear the birds singing. I didn't care about the dog poop we might be stepping in. I didn't really care about anything. I was holding my only remaining child, the joy of my life, in my arms. And I was frozen in time as the weight of Josh's death bonded us even closer. The weight of making decisions to stop life support. The weight of memories of all of Josh's life. The weight of realizing that no additional memories would be made with him. The weight of knowing she'd never see her brothers and I'd never see my sons, ever again. The weight was crushing. We hugged so tight.

And I cried.

AFTERTHOUGHTS

"How do you do it?"

"How awful to lose both your sons."

"I'll bet your glad you had three kids."

"No mother should have to see their son die, and you have outlived them both."

. . .

I got lots of statements and questions like that in the weeks following Josh's death. I'd tell people, "I don't know how I deal with it. I just keep moving on."

It's incredibly sad. That's for sure. Rick's death came as a total, complete surprise. He was doing so good. He was off all the hard stuff. He drank in moderation. Shucks he was planning to get married. He was so happy. But he drank enough to mess with his judgement when he dived into his swimming pool. I have often wondered what it was like for him to possibly be alert, realize he couldn't move, and know he would die. All in a matter of seconds.

Josh's dying was different. I anticipated it for years. In fact, I started writing his eulogy the day Rick died. I knew Josh was sick and getting sicker every week. He was so skinny. He lost so much strength as his muscles atrophied because of malnutrition. His brain told him he had to drink, that he needed alcohol. More than he needed food. One day a few weeks after the tornado, he watched me do my twenty-five pushups, something I try to do every morning. He giggled a little and made a joke about the way I was doing them – not exactly military style, but in my mind, pushups none the less. He got down on the floor and tried, but couldn't do even one. He couldn't push his shoulders off the floor,

125

much less his skinny little butt. I felt sad every time I saw him all last summer, and for years before that. So sad I had to work hard to fight the tears back nearly every time we were together. Sometimes I just could not look at him at all.

How could he not see what I was seeing in him? How could he not know that every drink he poured down his throat, and every cigarette he sucked down in his lungs was leading him closer to his death? I just couldn't imagine that he wanted to live that way. I wondered how he could even call it living, considering how active and vitally alive he used to be.

I told him once that my doctor advised me to not eat pizza, french fries, or fast food because my cholesterol was edging up. I didn't eat any of those things for three years. He wasn't impressed. Of course, if my doctor told me I could never have another drink, I'd have a hard time doing that. It's not that I drink a lot, it's just that it has been a part of my socializing since I was in high school. I can't imagine finishing a golf game on a hot afternoon and not cooling off with a cold adult beverage. Or going to a family get together, or watching a football game without it. Nope that would be very hard for me.

. . .

At the dinner at the Moose, one of my nieces asked me how I could possibly deal with all the trauma and loss I've been dealt. I responded, "When the kids were young, I prayed at the Offertory during Mass, 'Lord let me be salt of the earth and light to the world.'"

She said, "So you were asking for it, right?"

"I guess so. Once I figured that out, I prayed to be kind, and never say or do anything to cause harm to anyone." It's a good challenge for me.

. . .

I'm so grateful to be able to find comfort in what's left of my family. Joe continues to enjoy his work at the Moose. Not only does he help with administrative details, he really enjoys bartending,

As soon as he sees a member walk in, he gets their drink ready and puts a cold one in front of them before they even sit down. The one good thing that happened during the first tornado, was that part of the ceiling fell on Joe's shoulder and pulverized some bone spurs that had been bothering him for years. He was anticipating extensive shoulder surgery. But when he went to physical therapy after the tornado, he had full range of motion, and now no surgery is needed.

Gunner at age sixteen, continues to live with Joe, has the freedom of driving, and the responsibility of work. His thought processes are … interesting. He rationalizes wild and crazy things that benefit him in some thought-provoking ways. Man, he is fun to talk to!

Trevor continues to work towards total independence, which means I don't get to see him much because he works a lot of hours. He's front man in a band and is absolutely amazing in it. I don't understand their music, but I love watching him perform. He is so intelligent. He can talk to anyone for hours on any subject. He's quite the conversationalist.

Liza is more reserved, gentle, and loves cats. She doesn't like to be the center of attention. Also, highly intelligent like Trevor. Now in high school, she's enrolled in advanced classes. And like her dad, Josh, Liza loves to play softball.

Hunter and Riley have been living together since she got out of her most recent stay at Women's Recovery. This is so surprising to me because they fought like cats and dogs when they were kids. But, like she said in her journal, "Me and my twin always stayed together."

Hunter is in the Army National Guard. He called me a few weeks after Riley moved in with him. He vented about how Riley was so needy and she complained about having to sleep on the couch. He added, "She sure is high maintenance for someone who was homeless and slept outside on a park bench for seven months." OMG, I laughed so hard. He said no way did he say that to her.

They are both employed at the same meat processing plant. They work different shifts, so rarely even see each other. This just might work. They are so happy to be making money and taking care of themselves. Riley texted me the day after they bought something for the house they moved into: It felt so good to sleep in an actual bed!

Sophie and Jimmy continue to do well. They moved into a bigger house recently. As I was admiring the place, Sophie said to me, "You know Nanc, we'll always a place for you here, if you need it."

I was taken aback as I imagined that possible scenario. I paused a second, then said, "Soph there's no chance in hell that you would be able to take care of me when I'm old and can't take care of myself."

She got a puzzled look on her face. Then relief as she said, "Whew! Okay, good"

Their kids, Mikey and Megan, are a burst of fresh air to me every time I see them. I refer to them as M&M because they are bright and cheerful, and always fun to be around. They have they're mom's sense of humor.

Just this morning, I was talking to Sophie and told her that I reserved the niche next to Josh's at the cemetery. I added that it's not in anticipation of her need for a place through eternity, and that I kind of like the idea of me having a place with my boys, and a place near my own parents in our family plot.

Sophie thought for a minute, then asked, "How's that going to work?"

"What?"

"How are you going to have half your body cremated, and the other half buried?"

"No, no, no! I'll be completely cremated, then ashes separated. What are you thinking? Would I be sawed right and left sides, or top and bottom ends??"

A few minutes after we hung up the phone, I got a text from her: Mikey thought the same thing I did. Guts get buried.

* * *

Besides spending time with my family, it also helps me to talk about my book and my life to groups of people. I've given presentations at libraries with only three people in attendance. And I've spoken in front of high school groups as large as four hundred and some. Every group so far has been very attentive. Generally, the people who are there do not want to leave when I'm finished speaking. They seem frozen in time. It's weird.

I had to learn a lot about addiction to be able to speak to groups, because I do want to make a difference. I want people who are slithering away into an addictive state, to know they can get out of it. I want families of addicts to know that it is not their fault. Families need to make sure they are not enabling the addict by getting pulled into all the lies they will hear. Addicts need love and support no matter what they do or say. They already live with plenty of guilt and shame. And they pretty much hate themselves for the pain they live with, along with the pain they have caused their family and friends.

We all need to understand that addiction is a brain disease. It sometimes begins with self-medicating related to a mental illness, sometimes begins with "good times" partying, and sometimes when a person is trying to heal a broken heart. It always results in actual, detrimental changes to a person's brain. The brain in an addict tells the person to get more of the drug – *that's* what it needs. More than a job. More than shelter. Even more than food.

The brain can heal. The first thing that needs to happen is sobriety. And boy howdy is that hard! DT's in an alcoholic are exhausting. The anxiety and paranoia in a person coming off hard drugs is frightening. But with each passing day of sobriety, the brain is able to see clearer, make decisions more rationally. The neurotransmitters begin to work the way they were intended to work. Eventually, the addict will function more normally.

I've heard people say, once they've been sober for months to years, that they just can't believe what they did to themselves, and what they put their families through. I know several addicts in recovery who read my first book, *Destination ... Sanity*, and told me they had a hard time getting through it because of the old emotions it uncovered for them. All of them said they are so glad they got through their addiction and can now be sober in any situation.

Unfortunately, the urge will always be there to use again. The part of the brain that rationalizes continued use of their drug of choice, gets weaker as it heals. And the part of the brain that logically identifies that those drugs are harmful gets stronger. That takes more than sobriety and going to AA and NA meetings. It takes more than getting closer to a higher being. It takes more than being loved. It takes coming to grips with what you have done, forgiving yourself, and finally, starting to love yourself.

A friend of mine started drinking with her dad when she was in high school. After her first drink, she drank till she passed out. For years after that, every time she had one drink, she continued drinking till she passed out. She completed college and remembers little of it. She's been sober now for nearly forty years. And she realizes that it will only take one sip of one drink for her to be again need more alcohol and end up out of control.

Al-anon meetings have been helpful for me. Through them I learned to not be an enabler. I tried to help Rick when he first had the twins by paying their utility bills when they were broke. Retrospectively, I now know that what I really did was open their funds to buy more drugs and get high.

I also learned to distance myself from him. That was hard. Six years of not knowing where Rick was, or if he was dead or alive. Yeah. That was hard.

Fortunately, that distancing came more natural with Josh. It was automatic for me to kick him out of my house when I realized he was drinking there. No way could I abide by that while Riley was living with me. She was new at trying to be sober.

Families of Addicts (FoA) is a support group that started in Dayton, Ohio and they are spreading far and wide. Since addicts in recovery and families who have addicts in them are all together in the same room, I get a lot of different perspectives about addiction when I go to these meetings.

One thing I've noticed is the internal beauty and peacefulness of folks in recovery. Last summer FoA sponsored a festival of sorts on the courthouse square. It was so uplifting to be around people who beat their drug demons and remain sober. They sauntered about the thousands of people in attendance and were involved in meaningful conversations. They had all the time in the world. I stayed there a few hours then walked the several blocks to the Oregon District where there was a star-studded celebrity fun day whose purpose was to help the city's healing process after eight people were killed there in a mass shooting just a few weeks earlier. They seemed to be in such a hurry to get to the entertainment, and booze. The looks in their eyes were so different from the looks in the FoA crowd. These people didn't even seem to know they have a drug demon in control of their thinking, their action, their lives. They just wanted to drink up and party down.

* * *

I get a little jacked up about the way some people treat a person who has experienced the loss of a family member. It's one thing when it's an elderly parent, or someone who has had a chronic condition that ended in a painful death. Those deaths are more common, and in most cases more accepted.

It's quite another thing when it's a child. Youngster or adult. That is a rare occurrence, and a lot of people do not know what to say or do when they are around the surviving parent. There has been some variance for me related to this subject since each of my boys died. Some people go the other way when they see me approach. Some people just cannot talk about it, so they change the subject. Some people checked in on me a few times, then if I seemed OK, they pulled back. Some people think that after a few weeks, I should be "over it" and not need any special attention. Some people think that since my boys were close to forty when they died, it's not such a heartache. Some people say that it's not so bad for me since I still have another kid and now a bunch of grand kids. Well most of that is bologna. The death of my two sons will always leave me tottering on the edge of grief. I might not show it, but it hurts. Sometimes the grief gets close to paralyzing, and it's hard to move in any direction.

This past winter was hell. It was sooo dreary. Not snowy. Just cold and wet. I'm so glad Riley left Piper with me. Piper is such a comfort. I can tell her anything and she still loves me. It's not so much that she's deaf that makes her easy to talk to, or that she's a dog. It was just nice to have a warm body with me to make me feel good and encourage me to go for a walk. I smile every time I see her. Heck, I smile whenever I think of her. The gloomy days of winter would have been unbearable without her.

. . .

Sometimes it's hard to not wallow in the past. To not be upset that drug addiction and alcoholism found a place in my family. It sucked at least three of my offspring into it's dark, dank underbelly. It made them get used to its ugliness. And they eventually took comfort in it. Then it shook two of them out when it was done with them. Done and dead.

. . .

As I look to the future, I know there will continue to be sad days for me, as I continue to miss Rick and Josh. I imagine Riley will continue to have her struggles as she figures out what she needs to do to stay clean. She's intelligent, loyal, and loving.

She's got this!

What will be will be.

SCHOLARSHIP

A portion of the proceeds from this book will benefit the Grieshop/ Wissman Endowed Social Work Scholarship Fund.

To contact the author for more information about the book or the scholarship, email Nancy at grieshopnancy@gmail.com.

To give to the scholarship, contact:

The Wright State University Foundation
3640 Colonel Glenn Highway
Dayton, OH 45435-0001

Foundation Office: 937-775-4921

https://liberal-arts.wright.edu/connect/give-to-the-college

Thank you for your donation.

ABOUT THE AUTHOR

Nancy Grieshop currently lives in southwestern Ohio where she continues to work as an LSW Care Manager in a local hospital. She still loves to connect with patients and their families in their times of health crises and she is uniquely empathetic because of the many crises in her own life. She was a nurse for seventeen years before becoming a social worker. In more recent years she has become a funeral celebrant and she can officiate weddings. She also volunteers at Homefull where she is helping to get the first mobile grocery store in the United States fully operational.

Her desire in writing this book is to lend hope and strength to others who are dealing with addiction, those who have family members who are addicts, and professionals who work with addicts.

* * *

Please contact her at grieshopnancy@gmail.com to arrange for a book signing or live presentation – either in person or by zoom application. She'd love to hear from you.

* * *

Stay safe. Love more.